Jesus Did It Anyway

G. P. Putnam's Sons
New York

Jesus Did It Anyway

The Paradoxical Commandments
for Christians

KENT M. KEITH

G. P. PUTNAM'S SONS
Publishers Since 1838
Published by the Penguin Group
Penguin Group (USA) Inc., 375 Hudson Street, New York, New York 10014, USA · Penguin Group
(Canada), 90 Eglinton Avenue East, Suite 700, Toronto, Ontario M4P 2Y3, Canada (a division of Pearson
Penguin Canada Inc.) · Penguin Books Ltd, 80 Strand, London WC2R 0RL, England · Penguin Ireland,
25 St Stephen's Green, Dublin 2, Ireland (a division of Penguin Books Ltd) · Penguin Group (Australia),
250 Camberwell Road, Camberwell, Victoria 3124, Australia (a division of Pearson Australia Group
Pty Ltd) · Penguin Books India Pvt Ltd, 11 Community Centre, Panchsheel Park, New Delhi–110 017,
India · Penguin Group (NZ), Cnr Airborne and Rosedale Roads, Albany, Auckland 1310,
New Zealand (a division of Pearson New Zealand Ltd) · Penguin Books (South Africa) (Pty) Ltd,
24 Sturdee Avenue, Rosebank, Johannesburg 2196, South Africa
Penguin Books Ltd, Registered Offices: 80 Strand, London WC2R 0RL, England

Library of Congress Cataloging-in-Publication Data

Keith, Kent M.
Jesus did it anyway : the paradoxical commandments for Christians / by Kent M. Keith.
p.   cm.
Includes bibliographical references.
ISBN 0-399-15326-8
1. Christian ethics.   2. Altruism.   I. Title.
BJ1251.K36   2005   2005050901
241—dc22

Printed in the United States of America
1   3   5   7   9   10   8   6   4   2

This book is printed on acid-free paper. ∞

BOOK DESIGN BY AMANDA DEWEY

To Don Asman:

pastor, friend,

brother in Christ

Contents

Preface

I wrote the Paradoxical Commandments when I was a nineteen-year-old Harvard sophomore. They were part of a booklet that I created for high school student leaders titled *The Silent Revolution: Dynamic Leadership in the Student Council*. It was first published by Harvard Student Agencies in 1968. We sold or distributed about thirty thousand copies of the booklet between 1968 and 1972.

I went on with my life, and for twenty-five years I had no idea what was happening to the Paradoxical Commandments. I now know that during those twenty-five years, people were taking the Paradoxical Commandments out of my student leadership booklet and hanging them up on their walls, including them in speeches and articles, and passing them on to their friends. The commandments spread around the world, and today it is estimated that they have been used by millions of people.

The Paradoxical Commandments have been used in many ways by Christians all over the globe. They have been preached from pulpits, published in church newsletters, and posted on church and parish websites. They were used by Abel Muzorewa, a Methodist bishop who was the prime minister of Zimbabwe–Rhodesia. They were translated into Japanese and used in homilies by a Japanese Catholic priest in Tokyo. They appeared in the St. John's parish magazine in Wakefield, England. They were included in a student manual on morality and ethics published by the Canadian Conference of Catholic Bishops and a young adult Bible study curriculum published by the United Church of Christ. They were published in Dr. Robert H. Schuller's book *Turning Hurts into Halos,* Neil T. Anderson's book *Victory Over the Darkness,* and John Hagee's book *The Seven Secrets.*

In September 1997, I learned that the Paradoxical Commandments were published in a book compiled by Lucinda

Vardey titled *Mother Teresa: A Simple Path.* The Paradoxical Commandments were on the last page, before the appendix. They were given the title "Anyway," and were typeset to look like a poem. Vardey added a note at the bottom of the page, which said: "From a sign on the wall of Shishu Bhavan, the children's home in Calcutta."

I was deeply moved to learn that Mother Teresa thought that the Paradoxical Commandments were important enough to put up on the wall of her children's home in India. That discovery was a turning point in my life. It seemed to me that God was sending me a message. I felt called to speak and write about the Paradoxical Commandments again after thirty years had passed. Sharing the Paradoxical Commandments and their meaning became my lay ministry. I accepted invitations from all over the country to make presentations and give seminars on the commandments. I also wrote two books—*Anyway: The Paradoxical Commandments* and *Do It Anyway: The Handbook for Finding Personal Meaning and Deep Happiness in a Crazy World.*

As a result of my speaking and writing, which continue to this day, I have been getting messages from people all over the world, telling me how much the Paradoxical Commandments mean to them. I often hear from Christians who tell me how they use the Paradoxical Commandments in their churches, families, and individual lives. I am pleased to hear from all of them, and I am grateful that the Paradoxical Commandments are useful to them as they live their faith each day.

Many of the Christians who have contacted me have asked me to provide Bible stories and verses that illustrate the Paradoxical Commandments. They know that the commandments are based on Christian truths, but want to know how the commandments relate to the Christian faith and how they connect with scripture. Specifically, I've been asked to explain how they relate to the teachings of Jesus. I was first asked these questions at a presentation I made at the Hawaiian Islands Ministries Conference "Honolulu 2002," which was held to provide inspiration and resources for pastors and church leaders as well as lay Christians. More recently, I was asked these same questions by Dr. Robert H. Schuller of the Crystal Cathedral.

This book was written to answer these questions. It is for Christians who want to deepen their understanding of the Paradoxical Commandments through Bible stories and verses that illustrate them. It is my hope that in this way, the Commandments can serve as a daily reminder of the teachings of Jesus and the lives we are called to live as Christians.

I am not surprised that the Paradoxical Commandments have resonated with Christians. Jesus used paradoxes to teach us about the kingdom of God. His life itself was paradoxical. He was the Son of God, but he was born in a stable; he was the King of Kings, but he had no place to lay his head; he was the Savior who healed the sick and brought Lazarus back to life, but he himself died on a cross.

Jesus lived a paradoxical life. I believe that he is calling us to live a paradoxical life, too. This book is about the personal meaning and deep happiness that will come to each of us when we answer his call.

Jesus Did It Anyway

The Ancient Search for Meaning

I have met many people who are yearning for more meaningful lives. They want more meaning in their relationships with their families and friends, more meaning in their jobs, more meaning in the simple tasks of daily life. They know that a more meaningful life will make them happier, and they want to be happier—they want to be *deeply* happy. They want the kind of happiness that touches the spirit and connects with the soul.

I tell these people, You're right! You're looking for the kind of meaning you *should* be looking for. It's the kind of meaning God wants you to have. He wants you to have the

meaning that comes from living your faith, loving and helping others, and making a difference in your life and work.
And it's the kind of meaning that you *can* have. You just
have to know where to look and what to do.

We know from the scriptures that the search for meaning in life is not new. Unfortunately, people have often
looked in the wrong places. They have sought to find meaning in power, wealth, fame, and physical pleasure. But
power, wealth, fame, and physical pleasure offer little meaning. These things are only transient. And deep, lasting happiness doesn't come from the world around us. It comes
from our relationship with God.

That is the message in the Old Testament book of Ecclesiastes. It is estimated that Ecclesiastes was written during
the third century B.C. However, there is something strik-
ingly modern about the message of this book. Although it
was written thousands of years ago, it feels contemporary.
It is about the issues we face in our secular, commercial society *now.* The voice in Ecclesiastes said:

> I undertook great projects: I built houses for myself
> and planted vineyards. I made gardens and parks and

planted all kinds of fruit trees in them. I made reservoirs to water groves of flourishing trees. I bought male and female slaves and had other slaves who were born in my house. I also owned more herds and flocks than anyone in Jerusalem before me. I amassed silver and gold for myself, and the treasure of kings and provinces. I acquired men and women singers, and a harem as well—the delights of the heart of man . . .

I denied myself nothing my eyes desired;
  I refused my heart no pleasure.
My heart took delight in all my work,
  and this was the reward for all my labor.
Yet when I surveyed all that my hands had done
  and what I had toiled to achieve,
everything was meaningless, a chasing after the wind;
  nothing was gained under the sun.[1]

Ecclesiastes continues: "What does a man get for all the toil and anxious striving with which he labors under the sun? All his days his work is pain and grief; even at night his mind does not rest. This too is meaningless."[2] Money is

3

not the answer: "Whoever loves money never has money enough; whoever loves wealth is never satisfied with his income. This too is meaningless."[3]

Ecclesiastes reminds us that the world is not always fair or just: "In this meaningless life of mine I have seen both of these: a righteous man perishing in his righteousness, and a wicked man living long in his wickedness."[4] And life is unpredictable:

The race is not to the swift
or the battle to the strong,
nor does food come to the wise
or wealth to the brilliant
or favor to the learned;
but time and chance happen to them all.[5]

The word "meaningless" is used often in the translation of Ecclesiastes, but the word that is being translated, *hebel,* may also be translated as "like a breath," "transient," "fleeting," or "ephemeral." The message is that power, wealth, fame, and physical pleasure are short-lived. They aren't very meaningful, and they can't make us deeply happy.

What *is* meaningful? What *can* make us deeply happy? Ecclesiastes tells us that we should do good, find satisfaction in our work, and enjoy our daily food and drink.

> I know that there is nothing better for men than to be happy and do good while they live. That everyone may eat and drink, and find satisfaction in all his toil—this is the gift of God.[6]

Above all, we should revere God:

> *. . . Now all has been heard;*
> *Here is the conclusion of the matter:*
> *Fear God and keep his commandments,*
> *for this is the whole duty of man.*[7]

Our lives are a gift, given to us for only a short time. Power, wealth, fame, and physical pleasure are fleeting. But if we live in obedience to God, we will find deep happiness along with the confusion and pain.

The book of Ecclesiastes was written before the birth of Christ. The Messiah had not yet appeared. Centuries later, he came. Jesus brought new life, and new hope. He brought salvation. And he showed us how to find the kind of meaning and deep happiness that are not fleeting, but will last forever.

That's what this book is about: finding the kind of meaning and deep happiness that will last forever.

We will begin in the first chapter with the prayer of Jesus for his disciples during the Last Supper. In his prayer he recognized that his disciples were *in* the world but not *of* the world. To follow Jesus and find meaning and happiness, we, too, must be *in* the world but not *of* the world. Like Jesus, we must be *in* the world, loving and helping others, engaging the world and living full and faithful lives. But we do not have to be *of* the world. We do not have to seek power, wealth, or fame. We do not have to be fashionable. We do not have to conform to the ways of the world.

If we are *in* the world but not *of* the world, we can always find meaning, no matter how difficult or painful life becomes. This is the message of Good Friday, which we will explore in the second chapter. While suffering unimaginable physical pain, Jesus loved people *anyway.* He forgave people *anyway.* And he saved people *anyway.* Jesus showed us that no matter what the world does to us, we can find meaning in the way we *respond* to what the world does to us. We can respond in a way that is meaningful to us because it is consistent with our spirit and our faith.

The Paradoxical Commandments remind us to do the things that will give us meaning, even in the face of adversity. This book devotes a chapter to each of the commandments, explaining them in the context of the Christian faith. The commandments will be illustrated by stories from both the Old Testament and the New Testament, the teachings of Jesus and the apostles, my own life, and the lives of other Christians.

The final chapter is about making a difference. When we follow Jesus and *do it anyway,* we will not only find personal meaning and deep happiness—we will become the person God wants us to be, and we will make the difference that we were born to make. Our faith will flow into our deeds, and we will glorify God by loving and helping others.

But first, we must hear the call.

The Call

God loves us and wants us to be happy. Deeply happy.

But how can we be deeply happy in a world of conflict, pain, and disappointment?

By following Jesus.

How do we do that?

By being in the world but not of the world.

By loving and helping people, no matter what.

By reaching out to those in need and making a difference, now.

Jesus lived a paradoxical life.

He is calling us to follow him.

He is calling us to do it anyway.

In the World,
Not *of* the World

An idea that has given me strength and guidance over the years is the idea of being *in* the world but not *of* the world. I learned this from Jesus. At the Last Supper, when Jesus prayed for his disciples, he said:

"I have given them your word and the world has hated them, for they are not of the world any more than I am of the world. My prayer is not that you take them out of the world but that you protect them from the evil one."[8]

"The world" in these passages means the society or culture in which we live—the world of business, government, the military, schools, the media, and social institutions. "The world" is the material world, not the world of God and faith.

Jesus was *in* the world. He did not retreat to a mountaintop. He walked among us. He ministered to us. He taught, and healed the sick, and fed the hungry. He wanted his disciples to do the same. In his prayer, he said he did not want God to take his disciples out of the world—he just wanted God to protect them from the evil one.

As disciples of Jesus, we should be *in* the world, loving and helping others. As we minister to those in need, we will experience joy and sorrow, learn to forgive and be forgiven, and grow toward God.

However, while Jesus was *in* the world, he was not *of* the world, and he did not want us to be, either. In praying for his disciples, Jesus said that they were not of the world any more than he was. As disciples of Jesus, we aren't defined by the ways of the world. We don't have to have the same goals and lifestyles as the secular, commercial society that is all around us. We don't have to seek symbols of secular success like power, wealth, and fame. We don't have to be among the social elite. We don't have to live the way others expect us to live.

The point is not to be *against* the world. The point is that our faith isn't about secular, commercial success or social prestige. Our faith is about loving God and following Christ.

Paul reminds us that we shouldn't conform to the ways of the world. Instead, we should seek to understand God's will:

> Do not conform any longer to the pattern of this world, but be transformed by the renewing of your mind. Then you will be able to test and approve what God's will is—his good, pleasing and perfect will.[9]

When we are *in* the world but not *of* the world, we are free. We are free to be who *God* wants us to be, not who *the world* wants us to be. We are free to love God and others, and fulfill God's will for our lives, without worrying about what the secular, commercial world thinks of us.

People who are "of" the world are usually seeking power, wealth, and fame. Jesus did not seek those secular symbols of success. He did not come to be an earthly king, with political power and palaces and storehouses of earthly treasures.

At the very beginning of his ministry, Jesus went into the desert, where he was tempted by the devil. The devil offered him all the kingdoms of the world, with all their authority and splendor. Jesus refused to be tempted. "Worship the Lord your God, and serve him only," Jesus said in response.[10] His realm was not the kingdoms of the world, but the kingdom of God.

Jesus was very clear about worldly power. He gathered his disciples around him and said this:

> "You know that the rulers of the Gentiles lord it over them, and their high officials exercise authority over them. Not so with you. Instead, whoever wants to become great among you must be your servant, and whoever wants to be first must be your slave—just as the Son of Man did not come to be served, but to serve, and to give his life as a ransom for many."[11]

As for worldly wealth, Jesus said that "a man's life does not consist in the abundance of his possessions."[12] He said:

"Do not store up for yourselves treasures on earth, where moth and rust destroy, and where thieves break in and steal. But store up for yourselves treasures in heaven, where moth and rust do not destroy, and where thieves do not break in and steal. For where your treasure is, there your heart will be also. . . .

"No one can serve two masters. Either he will hate the one and love the other, or he will be devoted to the one and despise the other. You cannot serve both God and Money."[13]

One day Jesus was approached by a rich young man who asked Jesus what he must do to get eternal life. Jesus told him to obey the commandments. The rich young man said he had kept the commandments—what did he still lack?

Jesus answered, "If you want to be perfect, go, sell your possessions and give to the poor, and you will have treasure in heaven. Then come, follow me."

When the young man heard this, he went away sad, because he had great wealth. Then Jesus said to his disciples, "I tell you the truth, it is hard for a rich man to enter the kingdom of heaven. Again I tell you, it is easier for a camel to go through the eye of a needle than for a rich man to enter the kingdom of God."[14]

Jesus is not calling us to worldly power and wealth. He is not calling us to be "successful" in the worldly sense. He is calling us to follow him. If we do, we will be blessed. We will be blessed whether we are "successful" or not.

God has given each of us certain talents and abilities. When we use the gifts he has given us, we have the opportunity to glorify him. If we use those gifts well, we may be "successful" in the eyes of the world. If so, that success is simply a by-product of seeking to do God's will. If we achieve power, wealth, or fame, we know that they are simply tools to be used in serving God.

This way of viewing the world has made it easier for me to navigate the competing pressures and choices I have faced in my own life. I know that every day, the culture in which I live hammers home the idea that power, wealth, fame, and social status are the measures of success, and everyone should want to be "successful." But Jesus reminds me that those symbols of success don't matter. What matters is that I love God and help others.

When I choose a job, it should be the job that I believe I am called to do, not the job that offers the most power, wealth, fame, or social position. And I should not be afraid to take risks, or break social norms, when it is necessary to follow Jesus. I don't have to be "of" the world. I have to work hard, and use the gifts God has given me, but I don't have to work for the symbols of success. I just have to work for God.

The idea that we should not be *of* the world is a key to living the Paradoxical Commandments. Each commandment begins with a statement of adversity. Each statement about adversity is really about difficulties or failures in the secular, commercial world—the world of "success." Each statement of adversity is followed by a positive commandment, which is really about our spiritual lives—loving and helping others, and doing what is right and good and true.

The paradox here is that when things in the secular, commercial world are going badly, our spiritual lives can still be meaning-

ful and full of deep happiness. That is why Jesus does not want us to be *of* the world. He wants us to be free to grow spiritually and find deep happiness, no matter what the world does to us.

As we engage the world, loving and helping people, working and praying, we don't know what is going to happen. Why? Because we can't control the external world. We can't control the economy, population growth, the weather, natural disasters, international politics, war and peace. We can't control all the decisions made by governments and their citizens, or businesses and their consumers. A wide range of external factors can have an impact on us. We can work hard, and be prepared, and do our best to solve problems and seize opportunities. But we can't control the external world. That's why our spiritual growth and happiness can't depend on what the world does to us.

Deep happiness comes from our inner lives—our spiritual lives. That's the part of our lives that we *can* control. We get to decide who we are going to be and how we are going to live. That's our decision. And the good news is that we can decide to love God and each other, and live our faith, and live our most cherished values, and be close to our family and friends, and do what we know is right and good and true—no matter what. *No matter what.*

Jesus used paradoxes to help us see the kingdom of God. His paradoxical statements turned the secular world upside down. As we have already noted, he said that "whoever wants to become great among you must be your servant, and whoever wants to be first must be your slave."[15] He said that "the last will be the first, and the first will be last."[16] He said: "I tell you the truth, unless you change and become like little children, you will never enter the kingdom of heaven."[17] He said that "Whoever finds his life will lose it, and whoever loses his life for my sake will find it."[18]

Christians around the world cherish the Beatitudes that Jesus shared with his disciples as they sat together on a mountainside. You don't need to look too closely to see that the Beatitudes are paradoxical truths about the life of the spirit:

"Blessed are the poor in spirit,
*   for theirs is the kingdom of heaven.*
Blessed are those who mourn,
*   for they will be comforted.*

Blessed are the meek,

    for they will inherit the earth.

Blessed are those who hunger and thirst for righteousness,

    for they will be filled.

Blessed are the merciful,

    for they will be shown mercy.

Blessed are the pure in heart,

    for they will see God.

Blessed are the peacemakers,

    for they will be called sons of God.

Blessed are those who are persecuted because of righteousness,

    for theirs is the kingdom of heaven."[19]

Jesus did not say, "Blessed are the rich and famous . . . Blessed are the powerful and clever . . ." The Beatitudes are not about "success" in the material world. They are about the life of the spirit—the richer, deeper life of faith that Jesus offers each of us.

One of the most special moments in my life occurred in the Holy Land on "The Hill of the Beatitudes" near Capernaum. I was there with my family and members of my church. It was a quiet, sunny afternoon. We sat among the rocks and grass on the hillside. I felt especially close to my wife and children, and I thanked God for them. A member of our group read the Beatitudes out loud, and then we sang and prayed. I looked down the hill, across a bright green orchard, to the hazy blue Sea of Galilee. I felt an immense inner peace, a peace that is not of this world. It was the peace of God.

When we are *in* the world, but not *of* the world, the peace of God can be ours, every day.

The Message of
Good Friday

We know there is beauty and goodness in the world, but sometimes it is hard to see. Instead, we see only conflict and suffering. Every day, the newspapers report the beatings, the killings, the sickness and starvation, the inhumanity of human beings toward each other.

There are days when we feel overwhelmed by the cruelty and pain and hate. We wake up in the morning and find ourselves seized with despair. Everywhere we turn, we are greeted with bad news, unhappiness, and strife, and there seems to be no relief. We fear that no matter what we do, evil will ultimately prevail. Sometimes that fear is hard to shake, and it wears us down. We struggle to keep going, to keep believing in spite of our own doubts and disappointments. Amidst it all, we wonder: Does anybody understand what we are going through?

We know that the answer is yes. Somebody *does* understand. His name is Jesus, and he is the Christ.

Jesus suffered. He experienced cruelty and pain and hate. But he did more than that: He showed us how to *triumph* over the cruelty and pain and hate. He showed us that even in a world in which evil is strong, we can be who we are meant to be, and do what we are meant to do. He showed us how to rise above our fear and despair. He showed us how to live our faith and find meaning and deep happiness.

I did not understand this at first, because I didn't understand the message of Good Friday. All I knew was that Good Friday was painful. It hurt to think about what happened on that day two thousand years ago. I didn't like the fact that it was called "Good Friday." My question was: What's so good about Good Friday? It was such a tragic day. As far as I was concerned, it was the worst day in the history of the world. So I wanted to just skip over Good Friday and go straight to Easter Sunday. That was where I wanted to be—rejoicing in the resurrection, the glory of the risen Christ. But Friday? No. Friday was just sad and depressing.

Fortunately, it finally occurred to me, as it has occurred to millions of Christians, that I was looking at only part of what happened on Good Friday. Yes, it does hurt to recall how Jesus was beaten, and whipped, and mocked, and forced to carry the cross, and nailed to the cross. It does hurt to remember how he suffered and died on the cross.

But the story of Good Friday is not only about how the world treated Jesus; the story is also about how Jesus *responded* to the way he was treated. And his response was astonishing. It was breathtaking.

In the face of cruelty and pain and hate, Jesus loved people *anyway*. He forgave people *anyway*. And he saved people *anyway*.

What a powerful message! Even on the cross, suffering and dying, Jesus showed his love by connecting his mother with his disciple John. Even on the cross, suffering and dying, he saved one of the robbers who was crucified with him. Even on the cross, suffering and dying, he asked God's forgiveness for those who had crucified him. We all know those words: "Father, forgive them, for they do not know what they are doing."[20]

The loving, forgiving spirit of Christ triumphed over all that the world did to him. The world couldn't change who he was and what he came to do.

So what's so good about Good Friday? The answer is simple: Jesus.

On Good Friday, Jesus not only gave his life to reconcile us to God—he also demonstrated that our spiritual lives are not about how the world treats us. Our spiritual lives are about how we *respond* to the way the world treats us. If we respond the way Christ did, we will always find meaning and deep happiness. That is what he wants for us. Christ wants *his* triumph on Good Friday to be *our* triumph, too.

Jesus calls each of us, in our daily lives, to live our faith, and love God, and love each other, and do what we know is right and good and true—*no matter what.* If we are strong in our faith, the world can't change us. We can still be who we are meant to be, and do what we are meant to do. We can do it *anyway.*

Yes, living the Paradoxical Commandments is not easy. But if we ask for Christ's help, and pray, and study the scriptures, and participate in a fellowship of faith, we can do it.

It is my hope for you that living the Paradoxical Commandments will lead you to a new spiritual understanding and a strengthening of your faith. I pray that you will know, in your own life, the blessed triumph of the spirit that Christ wants for each of us.

Jesus *did it anyway.* We can, too.

The

Paradoxical

Commandments

People

are illogical,

unreasonable,

and self-centered.

Love them anyway.

For me, this is the biggest and most important challenge: Loving people even when they are difficult to love. It took me many years to discover that I can love someone with whom I disagree. I can even love someone who does things of which I disapprove. I know now that love is deeper and more meaningful than agreement or approval.

I have learned as a husband, parent, and friend that I can love unconditionally. This is the kind of love that holds together our families, friendships, churches, and communities. I can disagree with someone or disapprove of their actions, and I can let them know how I feel and where I stand. But I do not have to withhold my love. I can love people even when they are illogical, unreasonable, and self-centered. And I know that is what Jesus wants me to do.

Nobody is more important to me than my wife and three children. I would be the first to admit that we don't always agree. In fact, we have had some very heated disagreements. But I do my best to make it clear that I still love each of them, regardless of what I or they have done or not done, said or not said.

When my children were little, I used to tuck them in at night and say the words that my children referred to as "the nice words." Night after night, year after year, I knelt by the bed of each of my children and said: "I love you. You're a good kid. I like being your daddy. I'm glad you're my son/ daughter. I like being part of your family. And I hope you have a good night's sleep!" Then each daughter got a kiss on the cheek, and my son got a pat on the head, and I turned out the lights.

There were nights when I was really angry at my kids for what they had done that day. There had been name calling, or hitting and shoving, or dishonesty, or the shirking of chores. As I knelt by the bed, I talked to them about that, and made it clear that what they had done was wrong, and it was important that they not do it again. I talked quietly, but I made myself clear, so they knew I was unhappy. Then I would say "the nice words." Sometimes the words were hard to say, but I wanted them to know that even if I was upset with their behavior, I still loved them. I loved them *anyway*.

I kept saying "the nice words" year after year. Then the day came when our youngest daughter, Angela, let me know that she didn't need to hear "the nice words" anymore. I think what she meant was that she was a grown-up twelve-year-old now and "the nice words" were for little kids. I was surprised, but I said okay. Several nights went by without me tucking her in or saying "the nice words." Then one night when I was working at my desk at home, I heard Angela calling down the staircase to me.

"Daddy?"

"Yes, honey."

"Aren't you going to come up and tuck me in? You didn't say the nice words yet."

"Oh. Okay," I said. And the nightly ritual began again. She still wanted to hear the words, and I still wanted to say them.

✦ ✦ ✦

In the parable of the prodigal son, Jesus tells the story of a father who made it clear that he loved his two sons, even though each of them was illogical, unreasonable, and self-centered in his own way:

> "There was a man who had two sons. The younger one said to his father, 'Father, give me my share of the estate.' So he divided his property between them.
>
> "Not long after that, the younger son got together all he had, set off for a distant country and there squandered his wealth in wild living. After he had spent everything, there was a severe famine in that whole country, and he began to be in need. So he went and hired himself out to a citizen of that country, who sent him to his fields to feed pigs. He longed to fill his stomach with the pods that the pigs were eating, but no one gave him anything.

"When he came to his senses, he said, 'How many of my father's hired men have food to spare, and here I am starving to death! I will set out and go back to my father and say to him: "Father, I have sinned against heaven and against you. I am no longer worthy to be called your son; make me like one of your hired men."' So he got up and went to his father.

"But while he was still a long way off, his father saw him and was filled with compassion for him; he ran to his son, threw his arms around him and kissed him.

"The son said to him, 'Father, I have sinned against heaven and against you. I am no longer worthy to be called your son.'

"But the father said to his servants, 'Quick! Bring the best robe and put it on him. Put a ring on his finger and sandals on his feet. Bring the fattened calf and kill it. Let's have a feast and celebrate. For this son of mine was dead and is alive again; he was lost and is found.' So they began to celebrate.

"Meanwhile, the older son was in the field. When he came near the house, he heard music and dancing.

So he called one of the servants and asked him what was going on. 'Your brother has come,' he replied, 'and your father has killed the fattened calf because he has him back safe and sound.'

"The older brother became angry and refused to go in. So his father went out and pleaded with him. But he answered his father, 'Look! All these years I've been slaving for you and never disobeyed your orders. Yet you never gave me even a young goat so I could celebrate with my friends. But when this son of yours who has squandered your property with prostitutes comes home, you kill the fattened calf for him!'

"'My son,' the father said, 'you are always with me, and everything I have is yours. But we had to celebrate and be glad, because this brother of yours was dead and is alive again; he was lost and is found.'"[21]

The younger son had been illogical, unreasonable, and self-centered. He took his inheritance and then squandered it. But his father loved him *anyway.*

The older son was also illogical, unreasonable, and self-centered. He refused to celebrate his brother's return. He was self-righteous and could think only of himself. But his father loved him *anyway.*

+ ✦ +

Love is central to the teachings of Jesus. When asked by a Pharisee which is the greatest commandment in the law, Jesus answered:

> "'Love the Lord your God with all your heart and with all your soul and with all your mind.' This is the first and greatest commandment. And the second is like it: 'Love your neighbor as yourself.' All the Law and the Prophets hang on these two commandments."[22]

At the Last Supper, Jesus said:

> "A new command I give you: Love one another. As I have loved you, so you must love one another. By this all men will know that you are my disciples, if you love one another."[23]

Again, in John 15:12, Jesus said: "My command is this: Love each other as I have loved you." By commanding his disciples to "love each other as I have loved you," Jesus was giving himself as the model of the love that we are to show each other.

Perhaps Jesus' most extraordinary teaching about love is that we should love our enemies. In Matthew 5:43–48, Jesus says:

> "You have heard that it was said, 'Love your neighbor and hate your enemy.' But I tell you: Love your enemies and pray for those who persecute you, that you may be sons of your Father in heaven. He causes his sun to rise on the evil and the good, and sends rain on the righteous and the unrighteous. If you love those who love you, what reward will you get?"

The message is also found in Luke 6:32–36:

> "If you love those who love you, what credit is that to you? Even sinners love those who love them . . . But love your enemies, do good to them, and lend to

them without expecting to get anything back. Then your reward will be great, and you will be sons of the Most High, because he is kind to the ungrateful and wicked."

Jesus calls us to love people *anyway*. He didn't say that we should love each other only when we feel like it, or when it is convenient, or when the people we are supposed to love are charming and lovable. He didn't say we can give it a try, but if we get tired, or it doesn't work out, we can just give up. Jesus doesn't allow any excuses.

In the New Testament, there are more than twenty verses urging us to love others. Could God have made it any clearer? We are *commanded* to love people whether we like them or not. We must love people *anyway*.

Why? Because love is what the Christian life is about. It is why we are here. If we do not love others, we are not who we are supposed to be; we are not all that we can be; we are not doing all that we can do. If we do not love others, we miss God's purpose for our lives.

Even more important, if we do not love, we will not know God. As the apostle John wrote: "Dear friends, let us love one another, for love comes from God. Everyone who loves has been born of God and knows God. Whoever does not love does not know God, because God is love."[24]

We are built to run on love—God designed us that way. Loving and being loved are essential to our spiritual growth and happiness. Without love, our lives are meaningless. Paul reminds us in a well-known passage, 1 Corinthians 13:1–3:

> If I speak in the tongues of men and of angels, but have not love, I am only a resounding gong or a clanging cymbal. If I have the gift of prophecy and can fathom all mysteries and all knowledge, and if I have a faith that can move mountains, but have not love, I am nothing. If I give all I possess to the poor and surrender my body to the flames, but have not love, I gain nothing.

Love comes from God. He created us to love each other. When we do, God lives in us, and we find personal meaning and deep happiness at every turn. That's what Jesus wants for us. He doesn't want us to limit our lives by limiting our love. He wants us to love each other *anyway*.

> *People are illogical, unreasonable,*
> *and self-centered. Love them anyway*

If you do good,

people will accuse

you of selfish

ulterior motives.

Do good anyway.

Almost every day, I hear a friend, a colleague, or a news reporter casting suspicion on the motives of someone who is doing good. They imply that others who *seem* to be doing good are only *pretending* to do good when in fact they have their own selfish ulterior motives.

Many years ago I served as the president of a religious university. The university had an important mission and values, and the quality of teaching was excellent. Like other small private universities of the time, however, it was in dire financial straits, and was facing the loss of accreditation.

Experts who had visited the campus didn't think that the university would survive. I believed that it was worth saving, and I felt called to accept the job. It turned out to be the toughest, most agonizing challenge I have ever taken on. Fortunately, due to the efforts of many fine people, the university is now strong and thriving.

I remember that during my first week as president, a faculty member came to see me. He sat down and gave me a big, knowing grin. "I know why you took the job," he said. "You took it because it will be a good springboard. You plan to run for statewide office. This is just part of your plan to increase your visibility and position yourself to run."

I was truly surprised. Taking the job had been a big risk both personally and professionally. I accepted the risk only because I fervently believed in the university and wanted it to survive. However, I learned over the next few years that the faculty member who came to see me that day would never accept my explanation, because that is not how he saw the world. He interpreted the actions of others in terms of selfish ulterior motives.

David knew what it is like to be accused of selfish ulterior motives. When the Philistine and Israelite armies were drawn up for a confrontation and Goliath was taunting the Israelites, David's father sent him to the Israelite camp with food for his brothers and their commander. When David arrived and started asking questions about Goliath, his oldest brother, Eliab, became angry and said to him: "Why have you come down here? And with whom did you leave those few sheep in the desert? I know how conceited you are and how wicked your heart is; you came down only to watch the battle."[25]

David did what his father had asked him to do, but his brother accused him of being conceited and wicked, shirking his work to see the battle. David was accused of selfish ulterior motives. But it didn't deter him. He kept asking questions until he understood the situation. Then he went on to do good anyway. He volunteered to fight Goliath— and he won.

Later, when David was king, his son Absalom raised an

army to seize the throne from him. David fled Jerusalem with his officials and supporters. During his flight, he was accosted by Shimei, a member of Saul's clan. Shimei cursed David and pelted him and his officials with stones. "Get out, get out, you man of blood, you scoundrel! The Lord has repaid you for all the blood you shed in the household of Saul, in whose place you have reigned."[26]

David had been loyal to Saul and his son Jonathan, and had assumed the throne only after they had both been killed in battle. Now, after serving many years as a good king, he was being accused of being a scoundrel with selfish ulterior motives who had shed blood in Saul's household.

But David was not disheartened, and he continued to do good anyway. He could have had Shimei killed, but he let him live, saying: "It may be that the Lord will see my distress and repay me with good for the cursing I am receiving today."[27]

Psalm 109, attributed to David, includes these words:

O God, whom I praise,
  do not remain silent,
for wicked and deceitful men

> have opened their mouths against me;
>> they have spoken against me with lying tongues.
> With words of hatred they surround me;
>> they attack me without cause.
> In return for my friendship they accuse me,
>> but I am a man of prayer.
> They repay me evil for good,
>> and hatred for my friendship.

David called upon the Lord to help him as he faced wicked men and false accusations. He knew that the Lord would sustain him. Psalm 109 concludes by praising the Lord, "for he stands at the right hand of the needy one, to save his life from those who condemn him."

+ + +

Jesus was also accused of selfish ulterior motives. During his ministry, he healed the sick, fed the hungry, and reached out to comfort the outcast. He consistently helped others. He did good. But when the Jewish leaders took him to Pilate and Herod, he was accused of subverting the nation, opposing the payment of taxes to Caesar, and claiming to be king.[28]

The apostle Peter understood that when we do good, we may suffer. He said: "But if you suffer for doing good and you endure it, this is commendable before God. To this you were called, because Christ suffered for you, leaving you an example, that you should follow in his steps."[29] Peter encouraged us further with these words:

Who is going to harm you if you are eager to do good? But even if you should suffer for what is right, you are blessed. "Do not fear what they fear; do not be frightened." But in your hearts set apart Christ as Lord. Always be prepared to give an answer to everyone who asks you to give the reason for the hope that you have. But do this with gentleness and respect, keeping a clear conscience, so that those who speak maliciously against your good behavior in Christ may be ashamed of their slander. It is better, if it is God's will, to suffer for doing good than for doing evil.[30]

The choice is ours, and we should always choose to do good. Paul wrote to the Galatians: "Let us not become weary in doing good, for at the proper time we will reap a harvest if we do not give up. Therefore, as we have opportunity, let us do good to all people, especially to those who belong to the family of believers."[31]

People may accuse you of selfish ulterior motives. If they do, don't allow yourself to be distracted. As Psalm 37 says: "Trust in the Lord and do good." Be the person God wants you to be—a person who does good. That's where you will find personal meaning and deep happiness. That is where you will find Jesus.

> *If you do good, people will accuse you of selfish ulterior motives. Do good anyway.*

If you are successful,

you will win false friends

and true enemies.

Succeed anyway.

When you work hard and use the gifts that God has given you, you may become "successful" in the eyes of the world. One of the ironies of becoming "success-ful" is that you often become a target. Some people want to use you, and others resent your success and want to bring you down.

Isaac, the son of Abraham, was so successful that the Philistines became jealous. During a time of famine, the Lord appeared to Isaac and told him not to go to Egypt but to remain in Gerar, a town ruled by Abimelech, king of the Philistines. Isaac planted crops, and harvested a hundred times what he planted, because the Lord blessed him. He eventually became very wealthy, and had many flocks and herds. The Philistines became so envious that they filled up all the wells dug during Abraham's day. King Abimelech ordered Isaac to leave town, because he had become too powerful. Isaac moved away, and with the Lord's blessing, went on to become successful again.[32]

Samson is another example of someone whose success brought him the attention of those who did not wish him well. Samson was a renowned fighter and warrior leader. As a result, he won false friends and true enemies. But in the end, he succeeded anyway.

Samson's birth was foretold by an angel of the Lord, who instructed his mother never to cut his hair. Samson was to be set apart for God from the day of his birth. The angel proclaimed that Samson would begin the deliverance of Israel from the Philistines.[33]

Samson grew up to become very, very strong. The Bible says that he tore a lion apart with his bare hands. Later, he used the jawbone of a donkey to strike down a thousand Philistines. He went on to lead Israel for twenty years.

Samson fell in love with Delilah. The Philistine rulers approached her, offering to pay her to lure Samson into revealing the secret of his strength. Their goal was to overpower him, tie him up, and subdue him. Delilah wanted the money, so she asked Samson to tell her the secret of his great strength and how he could be tied up and subdued. Three times, he gave her false answers. But she continued to nag him, so finally he told her the truth: "No razor has ever been used on my head," he said, "because I have been a Nazirite set apart to God since birth. If my head were shaved, my strength would leave me, and I would become as weak as any other man."[34]

Delilah sent word to the Philistines, who came with the money they had offered. When Samson fell asleep on her lap, she called a man to shave off the seven braids of his hair. When Samson awoke, his strength—and the Lord—had left him. The Philistines seized him, gouged out his eyes, bound him with bronze shackles, and put him in prison.[35]

Delilah had become a false friend, and Samson was now in the hands of his true enemies. But he didn't give up.

The Philistines brought Samson from the prison to entertain them at the temple. All the Philistine rulers were there. Up above, on the roof of the temple, some three thousand men and women watched Samson.

Samson asked the servant who held his hand to lead him to the pillars that supported the temple. Then he prayed to the Lord, asking for strength just one more time. He reached for the two central pillars. "Let me die with the Philistines!" he said. He pushed with all his might, and down came the temple. In this way, Samson killed more enemies in his death than during his life.[36] Delilah betrayed him, and the Philistines blinded and imprisoned him, but Samson the warrior succeeded anyway.

+ ✦ +

Jesus, too, was successful, and he, too, won false friends and true enemies. As he traveled and taught, multitudes followed him wherever he went. Thousands gathered to hear him preach. He performed great miracles. He fed the hungry, healed the sick, restored sight to the blind, and cast out demons. He raised Lazarus from the dead.

In the midst of his ministry, Jesus won a false friend— Judas Iscariot, one of the twelve disciples. Judas betrayed

Jesus to the Jewish authorities for thirty pieces of silver. He led the Jewish guards to the Garden of Gethsemane, where he identified Jesus with a kiss.

We don't know what motivated Judas. Perhaps he wanted political change, and was disappointed that Jesus was not interested in becoming an earthly king who would overthrow the Romans and rule Israel. He may have thought that if he were arrested, Jesus would become "politicized" and take action. Perhaps he thought that if Jesus were questioned, he would persuade the Jewish leaders that he was indeed the Messiah. Perhaps it never occurred to Judas that Jesus would be killed. We don't know. In the book of Luke, we are simply told that "Satan entered Judas" and he went to the chief priests to discuss how he might betray Jesus.[37]

Later, Judas was sorry for what he did. After Jesus was seized, Judas begged the Jewish leaders not to harm Jesus. He returned the silver coins. And when it became clear that Jesus would die, Judas hanged himself in despair.

Judas was the false friend who started the chain of events that put Jesus into the hands of his true enemies. The scribes and Pharisees had been testing Jesus, and Jesus openly attacked their hypocrisy. As he performed more and more miracles, the Jewish leaders became concerned, and plotted to seize him. They were afraid to seize him out in the open, because he was popular and he was often surrounded by crowds. But the crowds were not there that night in the Garden of Gethsemane, and Jesus was delivered into the hands of his enemies. He was beaten, and whipped, and mocked. He was forced to carry the cross, and he suffered and died on the cross.

But Jesus succeeded anyway. He did what he came to do. He preached the gospel and healed the sick. He died for our sins and was resurrected. He reappeared to his followers to assure them that he would be with them forever. His disciples founded a church, and today there are two billion Christians around the world, worshipping Christ and seeking to follow him. A false friend and true enemies couldn't stop Jesus from changing the world.

✦ ✦ ✦

When you are successful, you may win false friends and true enemies. Why? There may be something about your success that will bring out the worst in others—those who are not successful, or who wish they could be more successful. Some may pretend to be your friends, when in fact they are simply trying to gain personal advantage at your expense. Others may become your enemies, because they may have wanted your success for themselves and are angry because they didn't get it.

Be patient with your false friends and true enemies. Treat them as potential allies. Keep the doors open to true friendship. Just because they see you as *their* enemy, does not mean that you have to see them as *your* enemy. They may be struggling with their own failures and disappointments. Their attacks may really be about them, not you.

Above all, cherish your relationships with your family and friends. Find the meaning and deep happiness that come from loving and being loved by people who will be by your side whether you are "successful" or not. When you are successful, they will be genuinely happy for you, and when you are not successful, they will be genuinely sorry for you—but they will always be there for you. Just make sure you are always there for them.

The false friend and true enemies of Jesus were all part of God's plan. Your false friends and true enemies may be part of God's plan as well. They may help you to become stronger in your faith and more like Jesus in your actions. So go forward, and use the gifts that God has given you. If you become successful, use your success to serve God. Whatever happens, stay close to your family and true friends, and remain faithful to your purpose, as God gives you the wisdom to understand it.

You are on this planet to love people and help people and make a difference. No false friend or true enemy should deter you from your purpose. They didn't stop Jesus. They shouldn't stop you.

If you are successful, you will win false friends
and true enemies. Succeed anyway

The good you do today

will be forgotten

tomorrow.

Do good anyway.

We never know whether the good we do will be noticed by others. Even if the good we do is noticed, it may not be remembered for long. Of course, we will remember, and God will remember. But everyone else is likely to forget. That shouldn't stop us from doing good.

The story of Moses is an amazing example. The good he did one day was forgotten the next. But he continued to do good anyway.

With dramatic help from God, Moses led the Israelites

out of Egypt and out of slavery. The Lord demonstrated his own power by causing a series of plagues to fall upon Egypt—plagues of blood in the Nile; then frogs; then gnats; then flies; then a plague on livestock; then a plague of boils; then hail; then locusts; then darkness; and finally, a plague on the firstborn. While these plagues devastated Egypt, the Lord protected the Israelites from harm. When Moses led the Israelites out of Egypt, God went ahead of them, guiding them with a pillar of cloud by day and a pillar of fire at night.[38]

It is hard to imagine a more dramatic demonstration of God's power and his love for the Israelites than this series of miracles. And there was no greater prophet than Moses. The Bible says:

> Since then, no prophet has risen in Israel like Moses, whom the Lord knew face to face, who did all those miraculous signs and wonders the Lord sent him to do in Egypt—to Pharaoh and to all his officials and to his whole land. For no one has ever shown the mighty power or performed the awesome deeds that Moses did in the sight of all Israel.[39]

But the Israelites had difficulty remembering what Moses had done for them. As they camped by the Red Sea, they saw the Pharaoh's army marching toward them, and they were terrified. They said to Moses: "Was it because there were no graves in Egypt that you brought us to the desert to die? What have you done to us by bringing us out of Egypt? Didn't we say to you in Egypt, 'Leave us alone; let us serve the Egyptians'? It would have been better for us to serve the Egyptians than to die in the desert!"[40]

Then the Lord told Moses to raise his staff and stretch out his hand over the sea to divide the water, so that the Israelites could go through on dry ground. The Israelites passed to safety, but the Pharaoh's army was swallowed by the sea. "And when the Israelites saw the great power the Lord displayed against the Egyptians, the people feared the Lord and put their trust in him and in Moses his servant."[41] They sang songs of praise to the Lord, exalting him.

But finding water and food in the desert was not easy. After three days of looking for water, the people were grumbling against Moses. So the Lord showed Moses how to make the bitter water of Marah sweet, and then led them to Elim, where there were twelve springs.

Later, they came to the Desert of Sin, where the grumbling against Moses and his brother Aaron continued. "The Israelites said to them, 'If only we had died by the Lord's hand in Egypt! There we sat around pots of meat and ate all the food we wanted, but you have brought us out into this desert to starve this entire assembly to death."[42] Then the Lord rained down bread from the heavens, bread that the people called "manna."

They continued to wander in the desert, stopping to camp at Rephidim. The people were thirsty, and again they complained. "They said, 'Why did you bring us up out of Egypt to make us and our children and livestock die of thirst?' Then Moses cried out to the Lord, 'What am I to do with these people? They are almost ready to stone me.'"[43] The Lord instructed Moses to strike the rock at Horeb with his staff, and water flowed from the rock.

Months later, in Sinai, Moses consecrated the people, and led them out of the camp to meet with God at the foot of the mountain. The Lord descended on Mount Sinai in thunder and lightning and smoke. The people were fearful, and stayed at a distance. When Moses spoke to God, the voice of God answered him. God gave the Israelites the Ten Commandments and other laws. The Lord made it clear that the Israelites should have no other gods before the Lord, and should not make idols and bow down to them.

The Lord told Moses to go up to the mountain and stay there, and he would give Moses tablets of stone on which were written the Lord's laws and commands. Moses stayed on the mountain for forty days and forty nights. The people grew tired of waiting for him to come back, so they gathered around Aaron and said: "Come, make us gods who will go before us. As for this fellow Moses who brought us up out of Egypt, we don't know what has happened to him."[44] Aaron told them to take off their gold earrings and bring them to him, and he made them into an idol in the shape of a calf. The people said, "These are your gods, O Israel, who brought you up out of Egypt."[45] Aaron built an altar in front of the calf. They held a festival with burnt offerings, and then sat down to eat and drink and indulge in revelry.

This made the Lord very angry, and he sent Moses back down with the stone tablets. When Moses saw the calf and the dancing, he was so angry that he threw down the stone tablets, breaking them into pieces. He burned the calf, and ground it into powder, scattered it on the water, and made the people drink it. Moses said that whoever was for the Lord should come to him. Those who did not come to him were slain, and the Lord struck the people with a plague in punishment.

And so it went. At each step in their liberation, the Israelites were grateful for the miracles of the Lord and the leadership of Moses. But then they forgot. They doubted God and Moses; they said it would have been better if they had died in Egypt. The Lord continued to manifest himself, but only forty days after God spoke to them in thunder and lightning from Mount Sinai, the people turned away from Moses and the laws of God and began worshipping a golden calf. The good that the Lord did was forgotten.

The same thing happened to Jesus. He taught, and healed the sick, and fed the hungry. He performed miracles. Crowds of people followed him wherever he went. On the day we celebrate as Palm Sunday, Jesus entered Jerusalem amidst the hosannas of the multitudes. The crowd went before him, spreading their garments and palm branches in his path, crying, "Hosanna to the Son of David! Blessed is he who comes in the name of the Lord! Hosanna in the highest!"[46] But the miracles that he had performed, and the good that he had done, were soon forgotten. A week after his triumphal entrance into Jerusalem, another crowd shouted to crucify him.

The Israelites forgot the good that God did for them, but God continued to be good to the Israelites anyway. Through Moses, he led them to the promised land and kept his covenant with his people. The crowds forgot the good that Jesus did, but Jesus continued to do good anyway. He suffered and died for our sins.

If people can easily forget the good that God does for them, why should we be surprised if people forget the good that *we* do? People easily forget. But their forgetfulness shouldn't change who we are and how we live. Who we are and how we live are more important than who remembers what we did.

Jack Brady understands that. Jack is a friend of mine

who lives his faith in daily ministry to others. His empathy and quiet encouragement have made a difference in the lives of people throughout his community. Years ago, he served as a county coroner and chaplain in Indiana. It was typical of Jack that he not only attended to the deaths that he was called to investigate—he also attended to the grieving families and loved ones left behind. It wasn't easy. What do you say to parents who have just lost a daughter in an auto accident, or whose son has just committed suicide? How do you comfort a wife who has lost a husband to a heart attack, or a husband whose wife has died of cancer? In his own unassuming way, Jack would ask if he could pray with them, and then he would share words of comfort and the assurance of God's love. Most of the people he ministered to were people he had never seen before, and would never see again. "I knew that whatever good I was able to do, it would probably be forgotten later," Jack says. "But when I saw their pain, I had to do what I could. I tried to do good anyway."

One day Jack found himself at a funeral for a man who

no longer had a family or friends to grieve his passing. Jack recalls:

I was called to investigate the death of a veteran of the armed services who died in his home. His service to his country had rendered him unable to cope emotionally. He lived on disability income and was an outpatient at a nearby Veterans Administration facility for veterans with special psychological needs. His next of kin was a brother who was in a nursing home in another part of the state. I talked to his brother's wife, who took responsibility for handling the funeral arrangements.

Two days later I saw in our local newspaper the notice of a graveside service scheduled for noon that day. I was running late on my way to the cemetery to attend the funeral, and I remember being worried when I drove up because I could not see the funeral tent. I hurried into the cemetery office to ask about the burial site, and was told that the funeral had not started and that it was a "drop-off." I didn't know what that meant, but I learned when I saw the funeral coach drive up. A "drop-off" is a funeral with just the funeral director, the cemetery director, and the VA chaplain.

As I stood at the gravesite I was really sad that this veteran had just been buried without a single family member or friend in attendance. I felt it was good that I was there.

Jack was the only one at the funeral whose job didn't require him to be there. He didn't have to attend. He knew that the veteran's family and friends would never know that he was there, and the officials who were there would quickly forget. But he went and did good anyway. He attended the funeral, and became the veteran's last friend on earth.

The simple fact is that it does not matter if the good we do is known or remembered by others. What matters is that we are children of God and disciples of Christ. What matters is that we do good, not for our own glory or prestige, but because that is who we are—people who serve God and do good. Paul reminds us that "we are God's workmanship, created in Christ Jesus to do good works, which God prepared in advance for us to do."[47] In doing good, we fulfill God's purpose and find new meaning in our lives.

> *The good you do today*
> *will be forgotten tomorrow.*
> *Do good anyway.*

Honesty

and frankness

make you vulnerable.

*Be honest
and frank anyway.*

In 1991 my wife, Elizabeth, and I adopted our two youngest children in Romania. During this process, Elizabeth had a crucial decision to make. She had to decide what to tell the Romanian Commission on Adoptions. She knew that if she were honest, we might lose one or both of the children we were adopting.

The Commission had recently decided that couples could adopt only one child, not two. But we were already in the process of adopting two when the Commission announced the new policy. We were already committed to both Angela and Spencer, certain that both of them were supposed to be our children. In fact, I had returned to the United States just a few weeks earlier to file amended paperwork so that we could adopt two children instead of one. Elizabeth had stayed in Romania to finish the adoption process.

The process grew more complicated when we learned that all the courts in Romania except those in Bucharest recognized the jurisdiction of the Commission. This was a problem for us, because Angela was in Bucharest, while Spencer was outside Bucharest, leaving us with one child on each side of the jurisdictional battle. While the Commission could not stop us from adopting Angela, we knew that it might decide to stop us from adopting Spencer when it learned about Angela. That would be a way for them to enforce their policy of allowing couples to adopt only one child. Meanwhile, if the Parliament amended the legislation that established the Commission, the courts in Bucharest could change their position on the jurisdictional issue, and the Commission could end up with the authority to stop us from adopting *both* Angela and Spencer. They might do that to punish us for trying to violate their policy by adopting two children instead of one.

It was a confusing time. The rules were not clear, there were conflicts in the information we were given, the situation seemed to change daily, and the future of our family was at stake.

The time came for Elizabeth to be interviewed by the commissioners to get their approval to adopt Spencer. She had waited for hours in the hallway just to get an appointment, and then discovered that the Commission didn't follow its appointment schedule. While waiting for her own interview, she saw more than one woman come out of the Commission office distraught and in tears because the Commission had denied her permission to adopt the child she wanted to adopt. The staff director, in particular, seemed to be using her authority in a heavy-handed way. There was no way to appeal a Commission decision.

What should Elizabeth tell the Commission? Should she be honest or not? Should she tell the Commission about Spencer only, or should she tell them about both Spencer and Angela? She decided to be honest. She knew it would make her vulnerable, and we might lose one or even both of our children. But she decided to be honest anyway. When she made the appointment with the Commission, it was in the name of both Angela and Spencer.

Finally, Elizabeth was called and was seated in front of the commissioners. She began by giving background information about our family. She provided the required documents—the financial statement, health statement, and home study. When asked if I also wanted to adopt the children, she passed around photos of me taken a few weeks earlier, smiling and holding each child. At that point, there was only one conclusion the Commission could draw: We wanted to adopt two children, in violation of their new policy.

Elizabeth held her breath, expecting a commissioner to ask the obvious question: "Why are you trying to adopt two children? You know our policy is to authorize only one. Pick one. You can only adopt one." But those words never came. The questions ended, and there was a pause. Then the Commission clerk turned to Elizabeth and said: "We will be happy to help you," and began filling out the authorization form.

Elizabeth was asked to wait outside while the clerk obtained a signature from the staff director. It wasn't over yet. The Commission had been willing to ignore the fact that we were adopting two children. Would the staff director do the same? Again, Elizabeth was left waiting in the hallway. Two hours later, her name was called. She looked up and saw that the clerk had a big smile on her face. The staff director had signed the authorization. Elizabeth had cleared a major hurdle in the adoption of our children.

For Elizabeth, honesty and frankness put our future family at risk, but she was honest and frank anyway. The commissioners respected her honesty, and decided to ignore their own policy and help us adopt both children.

+ + +

I admire the courage of Esther, whose story is told in the Old Testament. Esther knew that being honest and frank would put her life at risk, but she was honest and frank anyway.

King Xerxes banished his queen because she had disobeyed his command. His personal attendants then launched a search to find a beautiful young woman who would become the new queen. Esther, a Jewish girl who was "lovely in form and features," was an orphan raised by her uncle Mordecai. She was discovered during the king's search, and the king was so attracted to her that he set the royal crown on her head and made her queen. Esther did not reveal her nationality and family background to the king because Mordecai told her not to.[48]

Some time later, the king elevated a nobleman named Haman, giving him a seat of honor higher than the other nobles. The king commanded that the royal officials at the king's gate kneel down to Haman. But Mordecai, who sat at the king's gate, would not kneel. Haman was enraged. When he learned that Mordecai was Jewish, he determined to kill all the Jews throughout the kingdom. He obtained the king's permission to issue an edict in the king's name, and dispatches were sent out to the provinces ordering the death of all Jews, young and old, women and children, several months later.[49]

Mordecai sent a message to Esther, urging her to go to the king to beg for mercy and plead for her people. This was a risky thing to do, because according to the law, any man or woman who approached the king in the inner court without his permission would be put to death. The only exception occurred when the king extended his golden scepter to the intruder, a symbol that the intruder's life should be spared. Esther had not been called by the king for thirty days, and didn't know when she might be called again in the future. If she went on her own, and the king did not extend his golden scepter, she would die.[50]

Furthermore, Esther could not plead for her people without revealing her own identity as a Jew. If the king became angered by the revelation, he could banish her, as he had banished the previous queen, or he could simply make sure that Esther died with her people when the edict against all Jews was carried out.

Esther knew that being honest and frank would make her vulnerable. If she went to the king, revealed her identity, and pleaded for her people, she would be risking her life. But she put on her royal robes and went to the inner court. Fortunately, the king held out his golden scepter and welcomed her.

Esther invited the king and Haman to a banquet that day. During the banquet, the king's curiosity grew. What did Esther want? She said that if he and Haman would come to share a banquet with her again the next day, she would tell him.

After the banquet, Haman was in high spirits. He bragged to his friends and family about how he was the only person that the queen had invited to accompany the king to the banquet—and she had invited him to accompany the king to another banquet the next day. The only thing that made him unhappy was Mordecai, sitting at the king's gate. Haman's wife and friends suggested that he have a gallows built, and ask the king the next morning to have Mordecai hanged. Haman was delighted with the idea and had the gallows built.[51]

The next day, at the second banquet, Esther asked the king for her life and the life of her people. She told the king that she and her people had been sold for destruction and slaughter. The king asked who had threatened to kill them all, and she informed the king that it was Haman. When the king learned this, he decided to hang Haman on the gallows that Haman had built for Mordecai. The edict against the Jews was overturned, and Jews were given the right to assemble and protect themselves against their enemies. For Esther's people, it was a time of joy and gladness.[52]

By being honest about her identity and frank about the impact of Haman's edict, Esther made herself vulnerable. But she was honest and frank anyway. The result was that she saved herself and her people.

+ + +

Jesus was honest and frank, and it made him vulnerable, too. The gospel of John tells us that when Jesus was in the temple area walking in Solomon's Colonnade, the Jews came and asked him: "How long will you keep us in suspense? If you are the Christ, tell us plainly." Jesus answered, saying: "I did tell you, but you did not believe . . . I and the Father are one." And how did the Jews respond to this honesty and frankness? "Again the Jews picked up stones to stone him."[53]

Jesus continued to be very critical of the scribes and Pharisees, speaking openly about the way they behaved. He called them hypocrites, blind guides, snakes, and a brood of vipers.[54] He said:

"Woe to you, teachers of the law and Pharisees, you hypocrites! You are like whitewashed tombs, which look beautiful on the outside but on the inside are full of dead men's bones and everything unclean. In the same way, on the outside you appear to people as righteous but on the inside you are full of hypocrisy and wickedness."[55]

The scribes and Pharisees were stung by his words. They plotted to trick Jesus by asking him questions that would trap him into saying things that were treasonous or heretical. Before long, the Jewish leaders wanted him dead. They waited for the right time to catch Jesus and destroy him.

His honesty and frankness made him vulnerable, but even in the midst of the testing and threats, Jesus continued to be honest and frank anyway. We should be honest and frank, too. Of course, we should be polite and tactful when we share our truths. And we should remember that some truths should be spoken to only a few; some should be spoken in a confidential setting; and some truths do not need to be spoken at all.

Most important, when we are honest and frank, we should have the best interests of our listeners in mind. A useful guideline is a phrase from Paul: "Speaking the truth in love."[56]

I have learned that I cannot build strong, positive, caring relationships with my family, friends, colleagues, or those I serve unless I am honest and frank with them. I know that there are risks in doing this. When I am honest and frank with others, they may misunderstand me, or become uncomfortable with me, or even seek to retaliate against me. Being honest and frank makes me vulnerable. But it is worth the risk, because it opens the door to deeper, more authentic, and longer-lasting relationships. It makes it possible for me to better love and help the people with whom I live and work.

Honesty and frankness are the basis of trust. It is hard to build trusting relationships in our families, churches, and organizations if we are not honest and frank. How can we help and support one another if we are not honest and frank about our hopes, fears, strengths, and weaknesses? Paul knew this. He said: "Therefore each of you must put off falsehood and speak truthfully to his neighbor, for we are all members of one body."[57]

Sometimes, we need to be honest and frank enough to confront those we love with the truth about their behavior. Sometimes, they need to confront us about *our* behavior as well. While it is difficult to do, caring enough to confront can actually build a relationship. We are reminded by Proverbs 28:23: "He who rebukes a man will in the end gain more favor than he who has a flattering tongue." The reason is that honesty and frankness can help us grow, and connect with others, and build a depth of fellowship that flattery can never achieve.

Honesty and frankness, even when spoken in love, can make us vulnerable. Sometimes, people will retaliate. We need to pray and seek guidance before we speak. We need to be discerning. But there are times when we must be honest and frank, or we are no longer authentic, no longer disciples of Christ. We must stand and speak the truth in love, no matter how vulnerable it makes us. When we do, we will find personal meaning and inner peace.

Honesty and frankness make you vulnerable.
Be honest and frank anyway.

The biggest men and women

with the biggest ideas can be

shot down by the smallest

men and women with

the smallest minds.

Think big anyway.

Big men and women with big ideas make small men and women with small minds very uncomfortable and jealous. By "small men and women" I don't mean "bad" people, I mean men and women of any background or station in life who can't see beyond their own world—and their own world is small. Throughout history, people who think small have misunderstood and even persecuted people who think big.

When I was growing up, one of my heroes was Albert Schweitzer, who was born in 1875 in Alsace. After achieving fame throughout Europe as a brilliant musician, philosopher, and theologian, he decided to dedicate himself to serving humanity. At age thirty he began training as a doctor, and at age thirty-eight he and his wife went to Western Africa to serve the poor. His dream was to establish a hospital that would serve thousands of Africans.

In one of his books, Schweitzer told about his difficulty in getting help while constructing the hospital. His foreman for the construction work was a promising young man who was told by others that he was too talented to do manual labor, so he left Schweitzer to go to school instead. Schweitzer had to turn away from his work as a doctor to take the young man's place, organizing the lumber and bamboo, and wielding a hammer and saw.

As the rainy season began, everyone knew that they had to get the timber under cover, but few were willing to help. Schweitzer saw an African in white clothing sitting by one of the patients, whom he had come to visit. Schweitzer called out to him and asked for help. "I am an intellectual, I don't drag timber," the man replied. So Schweitzer, one of the greatest intellectuals of his time, had to drag the timber by himself.[58] A big man, with a big idea, was shot down by small men with small minds. But Schweitzer continued to think big anyway. He got the hospital built, and later moved it to another site, where he built a bigger one.

Men and women with small minds don't like people who have higher standards or a stronger faith. Daniel is an Old Testament example. Daniel was one of the three top administrators of King Darius. He distinguished himself by his exceptional qualities. He was so good, in fact, that the king was going to put him in charge of the whole kingdom. That stirred the ire of small-minded administrators and subordinates. They wanted to find fault with Daniel, but they couldn't, because he was honest and trustworthy. All they could find to attack was his faith in God. So they persuaded the king to issue a decree that anyone who prayed to any god or man except the king would be thrown into the lion's den. After the king issued the decree, they caught Daniel praying to God.[59]

The king was very distraught about this. He didn't want to order Daniel to be thrown into the lion's den. But the small-minded subordinates argued that the king couldn't change his decree. Reluctantly, the king allowed Daniel to be thrown to the lions.

The king returned to his palace, but that night he could

not eat or sleep. In the morning, he rushed to the lion's den and called to Daniel. He was overjoyed to hear Daniel answer:

"O king, live forever! My God sent his angel, and he shut the mouths of the lions. They have not hurt me, because I was found innocent in his sight. Nor have I ever done any wrong before you, O king."[60]

Daniel was not only still alive, he even managed to escape injury. The king was so impressed that he decreed that people throughout his kingdom must fear and revere the God of Daniel.[61]

Daniel was shot down by small men with small minds, but it didn't change him or his faith. He trusted the Lord. The Lord saved him, and he continued to serve God and think big.

Big ideas are usually about doing something new or different, and making things better. Small men and women feel so threatened by change that they don't want things to get better, because to get better, things would have to change. They believe that the old ways are always best.

Jesus came to bring the new gospel, and he, too, was shot down by small men with small minds. In fact, he was rejected in his own hometown of Nazareth. He went to Nazareth and began teaching the people in their synagogue. The people were amazed—and offended. How could Jesus have such wisdom and miraculous powers when he was just the local carpenter's son? In the gospel of Luke, we learn that the people in the synagogue were so furious with Jesus that they "drove him out of the town, and took him to the brow of the hill on which the town was built, in order to throw him down the cliff."[62] Jesus walked right through the crowd and got away. But he didn't do many miracles there, because of their lack of faith.[63] Of course, this didn't stop Jesus. He continued to think big anyway.

If the big ideas of a faithful servant like Daniel and the Son of God himself were shot down by small minds, we should expect that our big ideas will be shot down, too. But it shouldn't stop us—we should think big anyway.

We should think about how we can meet everyone's basic needs—food, clothing, shelter, health care, education, and jobs. We should think about what we can do to put an end to wars and diseases. We should think about the steps we can take so justice will prevail. We should think about how we can help love and understanding to flourish between people around the globe. Every step we take toward achieving these big ideas will be meaningful.

There are those who say that these big ideas cannot be achieved. There are those who will try to shoot us down. But Jesus didn't teach us about limits. He taught us to move mountains. We must keep our eyes on him, and think big anyway.

The biggest men and women with the biggest
ideas can be shot down by the smallest men and
women with the smallest minds.
Think big anyway.

People favor

underdogs, but

follow only top dogs.

Fight for a few underdogs anyway.

Most of us sympathize with underdogs. We know that they struggle. We know that the odds are against them. We'd like to see them win, but we rarely reach out and help them. Instead, we play it safe. We follow the top dogs.

Jesus was different. He truly cared about underdogs. He ministered to them. He invited them to a new life.

Jesus reached out to the poor. He healed lepers, epileptics, and paralytics. He healed the lame, the crippled, the dumb, and the blind. He exorcised demons. He forgave a prostitute.

Tax collectors were hated in those days. But Jesus called

Matthew, a tax collector, to follow him. Then he went to have a meal in Matthew's house.

> While Jesus was having dinner at Matthew's house, many tax collectors and "sinners" came and ate with him and his disciples. When the Pharisees saw this, they asked his disciples, "Why does your teacher eat with tax collectors and 'sinners'?" On hearing this, Jesus said: "It is not the healthy who need a doctor, but the sick. But go and learn what this means: 'I desire mercy, not sacrifice.' For I have not come to call the righteous, but sinners."[64]

Jesus came to reach out to those who needed him the most—the underdogs. He was not concerned with their social status. If they believed, they would be saved. Jesus knew that many people of low social status would be saved, and many of high social status would not. He told the parable of the two sons:

> "There was a man who had two sons. He went to the first and said, 'Son, go and work today in the vineyard.'

"'I will not,' he answered, but later he changed his mind and went.

"Then the father went to the other son and said the same thing. He answered, 'I will, sir,' but he did not go.

"Which of the two did what his father wanted?"

"The first," they answered.

Jesus said to them, "I tell you the truth, the tax collectors and the prostitutes are entering the kingdom of God ahead of you. For John came to you to show you the way of righteousness, and you did not believe him, but the tax collectors and the prostitutes did. And even after you saw this, you did not repent and believe him."[65]

When we care for the underdogs, we are caring for Jesus. That is the message of the parable of the sheep and the goats. Jesus said:

"When the Son of Man comes in his glory, and all the angels with him, he will sit on his throne in heavenly glory. All the nations will be gathered before him, and he will separate the people one from another as a shepherd separates the sheep from the goats. He will put the sheep on his right and the goats on his left.

"Then the King will say to those on his right, 'Come, you who are blessed by my Father; take your inheritance, the kingdom prepared for you since the creation of the world. For I was hungry and you gave me something to eat, I was thirsty and you gave me something to drink, I was a stranger and you invited me in, I needed clothes and you clothed me, I was sick and you looked after me, I was in prison and you came to visit me.'

"Then the righteous will answer him, 'Lord, when did we see you hungry and feed you, or thirsty and give you something to drink? When did we see you a stranger and invite you in, or needing clothes and clothe you? When did we see you sick or in prison and go to visit you?'

"The King will reply, 'I tell you the truth, whatever you did for one of the least of these brothers of mine, you did for me.'

"Then he will say to those on his left, 'Depart

from me, you who are cursed, into the eternal fire prepared for the devil and his angels. For I was hungry and you gave me nothing to eat, I was thirsty and you gave me nothing to drink, I was a stranger and you did not invite me in, I needed clothes and you did not clothe me, I was sick and in prison and you did not look after me.'

"They also will answer, 'Lord, when did we see you hungry or thirsty or a stranger or needing clothes or sick or in prison, and did not help you?'

"He will reply, 'I tell you the truth, whatever you did not do for one of the least of these, you did not do for me.'

"Then they will go away to eternal punishment, but the righteous to eternal life."[66]

This parable is a powerful reminder that we should serve those in need. Those who will enter the kingdom and be saved are those who feed the hungry, give drink to the thirsty, show hospitality to strangers, provide clothing to the naked, look after the sick, and visit those in prison. We also need to remember that serving those in need is serving

Jesus. "Whatever you did for one of the least of these brothers of mine, you did for me!"[67]

✦ ✦ ✦

Utu Langi knows what it means to be down and out. He was raised in Tonga, and then moved to the United States, where he found some childhood friends. Unfortunately, those childhood friends were dealing drugs, and he joined them. He was eventually caught, and was sent to prison to await trial on drug charges. He was facing a combined forty-five-year prison sentence. His wife was about to leave him, taking their two children with her. When the charges against him were dropped on a technicality, he knew it was a miracle. "The Lord in his mercy granted me a new life," he says. He gave his new life to Jesus.

Utu takes the parable of the sheep and the goats seriously. He and his fellow volunteers at the First United Methodist Church in Honolulu deliver blankets and food to thousands of homeless people each month.

It all began a few years ago, when Utu was driving home after working on the graveyard shift. He is a carpenter by trade, and he was doing renovation work at a hospital. As he drove through town, he saw a man at a bus stop. "He was alone, and I could tell he was cold," recalls Utu. "I had a blanket that I used to cover my tools, and as I drove by, I debated with myself: Should I stop and give him my blanket? Should I do what Jesus would do?"

Utu drove past, but then changed his mind and went back. He pulled his truck up to the bus stop, took out the blanket, and approached the man. "I asked him if he was cold, and then I realized that was a dumb question. So I just gave him the blanket. He didn't say anything, but the look he gave me was enough. I cried all the way home, just thinking about him."

Utu told the story to the pastor at his church. The pastor suggested he make an announcement during the Sunday service, asking for more blankets. "We collected twenty-two blankets that first time," Utu said. "We took them downtown, and within fifteen minutes we had given them all away to people who needed them."

Then one day he was reading the newspaper, and his two sons saw a picture of a little boy in Sudan. "There was a famine there, and the picture showed a little boy starving, crying, with flies all over his face," Utu recalls. "My three-year-old son wanted to know what was wrong with the little boy. That question haunted me all day. I told my wife we had to do something." They wrote to a number of churches and raised money for the hungry children of Sudan.

One night, when Utu was giving a homeless woman a blanket, she said she was very grateful, but what she really needed was some food. "That's when it hit me that we have people who are starving right here in our own town," said Utu. "And a lot of them were the same homeless people we had been giving blankets to."

Utu and his fellow volunteers began doing yard work to earn money to buy food for the homeless. They barbecued at a popular local beach park, and invited homeless people to come and eat. "We offered them food, and told them that God loves them." Within a year they were offering food at ten sites, and serving 12,000 meals a month to nearly 3,000 homeless people all over the island.

"There are lots of headaches," said Utu. "Organizing volunteers and keeping it all going can get messy. And we don't know where the next dollar is coming from. All we know is that the Lord has blessed us and this ministry. We keep working and sharing the good news about the Lord, and donors and resources keep showing up."

Utu's faith and his experience in working with the homeless have led him to want to know all he can about Jesus. He hopes to go to seminary someday. "I'm still learning from Jesus," he says. "But I am sure in my heart that our outreach ministry is the kind of thing he wants us to do."

+ ✦ +

It is much easier to follow the top dogs than to fight for the underdogs. Top dogs are popular, and following them is fashionable. We are attracted by their power, wealth, and fame. We know that following them is "safe." Fighting for underdogs, on the other hand, is risky. Underdogs don't have power, wealth, and fame. Instead, they may live in poverty, with limited access to education and health care. They may suffer from racial discrimination. They may struggle with physical disabilities. Standing up for underdogs means risking failure or disapproval. Fighting for underdogs can make *us* underdogs, too.

But if we love Jesus and seek to follow him, there is no

other way. His ministry focused on the underdogs. We must do the same. We will find great meaning and deep happiness when we follow in his footsteps and minister to those who need us the most.

People favor underdogs, but follow only top dogs.
Fight for a few underdogs anyway.

What you spend years

building may be

destroyed overnight.

Build anyway.

Most of us spend years building up our resources—our possessions, our homes, our businesses, our bank accounts. We nurture our families and try to take care of our health. While doing it, we know that any or all of it can be taken away by a fire or a flood, a change in the marketplace, an economic depression, an auto accident, or a sudden illness.

What would it be like to lose everything all at once—family, wealth, and health? It happened to Job.

In the Old Testament, Job is described as a blameless and upright man who feared God and shunned evil. He was the greatest man in his region. He had ten children and many servants. He owned thousands of sheep, camels, oxen, and donkeys. He had it all.[68]

Then Job lost it all. He lost everything he had built during his lifetime. And he lost it overnight.

It began one day when Satan appeared before the Lord. The Lord asked him where he had been, and Satan said he had been roaming the earth. The Lord asked Satan if he had considered his servant Job, who was blameless and upright, and feared God. Satan challenged the Lord. He said that if he took away everything that Job had, Job would curse the Lord. So the Lord agreed to test Job.

Soon, a messenger came to Job, informing him that enemies had carried off his oxen and donkeys and killed his servants. Another messenger told him that the fire of God had fallen from the sky and burned his sheep and his servants. A third messenger arrived to tell him that enemy raiders had taken his camels and his servants. A fourth messenger told him that his sons and daughters were killed when a mighty wind collapsed the house in which they were staying.

Job tore his robe and shaved his head, and then fell to the ground in worship, saying:

"Naked I came from my mother's womb,
   and naked I will depart.
The Lord gave and the Lord has taken away;
   may the name of the Lord be praised."[69]

Job remained faithful.

Then Satan spoke to the Lord again, saying that if you strike a man's flesh and bones, then surely he would curse the Lord. So Satan afflicted Job with painful sores from the soles of his feet to the top of his head. His wife said to him, "Are you still holding on to your integrity? Curse God and die!"[70]

But Job did not curse God and die. He asked his wife: "Shall we accept good from God, and not trouble?"[71] Job cursed his fate, but he didn't curse God. He was bitter about his suffering, but he did not turn against the Lord. Instead, he argued his innocence, and asked the Lord for deliverance.

Job passed the test. The Lord made him prosperous again, doubling what he had before. Once again, Job had sheep, and camels, and oxen, and donkeys. And he had seven sons and three daughters. Job built a new life. He lived to be 140, and saw his children and their children to the fourth generation.

+ ✦ +

After his conversion, Paul devoted his life to spreading the gospel of Christ and establishing churches throughout the land. However, he experienced some reversals along the way. For example, he spent a year and a half establishing a church in Corinth, one of the largest cities of his day.[72] Later, after he left Corinth, news reached him regarding problems in the Corinthian church. The church had become divided. There was jealousy and envy. Members of the church were having marital problems, and acts of sexual immorality were committed. Members were suing each other in pagan courts. The Lord's Supper was being misused, and members of the church were teaching against the resurrection of the dead. False prophets appeared, challenging Paul's teachings.

Paul must have been discouraged. The church of Corinth was in disarray. What he had spent so much time building had fallen apart. But Paul kept on building the church anyway. He wrote letters to the Corinthians to correct their behavior and inspire them to new levels of faith and understanding. The first of those letters, 1 Corinthians, includes beautiful words about love and resurrection—words that Christians all over the world cherish today.[73]

Like Job, we, too, may suffer. Like Paul, we, too, may lose what we have spent years building. But we can still affirm the glory of God, and build again.

Calamities are tests. They force us to think about who we really are and what is really important to us. They also force us to consider what kind of relationship we have with God.

We can find meaning and deep happiness by keeping a strong relationship with the Lord, no matter what. We can maintain our spirit and our integrity in the face of whatever calamity or disappointment comes our way. Whatever the world does to us, we can still love God, and we can still be who we are supposed to be.

And while we struggle with the pain of loss, we know our memories of what we built will always be with us, long after the things we built have faded or fallen apart. We can always cherish our memories.

When we suffer a loss and then build again, we demonstrate that our spirit and our relationship with God are stronger than any calamity or disaster. Tragedy is temporal; our faith is eternal. We suffer, but we go on. We praise God, and we build again. The joy is in the building.

What you spend years building may be
destroyed overnight. Build anyway.

People really need help

but may attack you

if you do help them.

Help people anyway.

It is confusing and frustrating to be attacked by people you are trying to help. It doesn't make sense. Why are they attacking you? At least your intentions are good—you're trying to help them. And if you are providing the help they really need, how can they be so ungrateful?

We know from the story of Saul and David in the Old Testament that this is not a new problem. When King Saul lost God's favor, an evil spirit tormented him. He asked his attendants to find someone who could play the harp for him, to soothe him. One of the servants knew of David, a brave young man, handsome and well spoken. Saul sent for him and took him into his service. When Saul was troubled, David played his harp, and Saul found relief. The evil spirit left him.[74]

One day the Philistines gathered their forces, and Saul and the Israelites went to meet them in battle. A Philistine champion named Goliath, who was over nine feet tall, challenged the Israelites to choose a man to fight him. If Goliath won, the Israelites would become Philistine subjects; if an Israelite won, the Philistines would become Israelite subjects.

The Israelites were terrified. No one would step forward to fight Goliath. For forty days, Goliath taunted them every morning and every evening.

David convinced Saul to let him fight Goliath. With a staff, five smooth stones from the stream, and a sling, David faced the huge Philistine. As Goliath moved to attack him, David ran to the battle line, slung a stone, and struck Goliath on the forehead. Goliath fell to the ground. David quickly drew Goliath's sword and killed him.[75]

It was an amazing victory. A young man armed only with a sling had defeated a giant in armor.

Saul really needed help—first with the evil spirit, and then with Goliath. David helped him by playing his harp and then defeating the giant. Saul was grateful. He kept David with him and gave him a high position in the army.

But soon Saul was filled with jealousy, and he turned on David. He told his son Jonathan and his attendants to kill David. David escaped, but Saul hunted him, intent on killing him.

Saul's son Jonathan was David's friend. Jonathan intervened on David's behalf, telling his father:

> "Let not the king do wrong to his servant David; he has not wronged you, and what he has done has benefited you greatly. He took his life in his hands when he killed the Philistine. The Lord won a great victory for all Israel, and you saw it and were glad. Why then would you do wrong to an innocent man like David by killing him for no reason?"[76]

Saul welcomed David back into his house, but his jealousy grew strong again. While David was playing his harp, Saul tried to pin him to the wall with his spear. Again, David escaped, and Saul continued to hunt him so that he could kill him.

Twice, David had the opportunity to kill Saul. Once, in a cave, David was so close to Saul that he was able to cut off the corner of Saul's robe unnoticed. Another time, he entered Saul's camp at night, crept to where Saul was sleeping, and took the king's spear and water jug that were near his head. Each time David spared Saul's life, and then confronted Saul to remind him that he intended him no harm. David said to Saul:

"Now understand and recognize that I am not guilty of wrongdoing or rebellion. I have not wronged you, but you are hunting me down to take my life. May the Lord judge between you and me. And may the Lord avenge the wrongs you have done to me, but my hand will not touch you."[77]

Each time David spared his life, Saul admitted that he was wrong about David. He told David that he should be rewarded and blessed. But Saul could not control his jealousy. Saul still wanted to kill David, so David remained on the run.

Saul really needed help, but he attacked David when

David helped him. David continued to be loyal to Saul anyway. He gathered a small army and fought the Philistines on his own. Later, when Saul and his son Jonathan died in battle, David lamented their loss.

+ ✦ +

Jesus wanted to help the Jewish leaders and Pharisees who had become self-righteous and self-important, focusing on fulfilling the letter but not the spirit of God's law. He wanted them to truly love God and their neighbors, forgive others, be humble in their worship, trust the Lord, and experience the joy of the kingdom of God. When they did not understand his message, he used blunt words to jolt them out of their complacency. Rather than opening their hearts to his message, they became more haughty and outraged, and plotted to kill him.

But some of them did get the message. For example, Nicodemus recognized that Jesus was a teacher who came from God.[78] John's gospel reveals that many of the Jewish leaders believed in Jesus, but because of the Pharisees, they would not confess their faith, for fear that they would be put out of the synagogue.[79] And in a dialogue between Jesus and a Pharisee about the greatest commandments, the Pharisee agreed with Jesus, saying that the two commandments—to love God and love your neighbor as yourself—were more important than all burnt offerings and sacrifices. Jesus acknowledged the wisdom of the man's answer. "You are not far from the kingdom of God," Jesus told him.[80]

But most of the leaders and Pharisees did not get the message. They really needed help, but when Jesus tried to help them, they attacked him. He continued to try to help them anyway.

Why would anyone who needs help attack us when we do help them? We know that some people need help but deny it. Others know they need help and resent it. Still others need help but aren't sure what help they need. As a result of their vulnerability or confusion, they may attack us when we try to help them.

But when they attack us, their attacks may not really be about us. Instead of being angry at us, they may really be angry about life. They may be suffering anguish about their helplessness. Whatever the reason, their attacks should not change who we are.

Of course, we must be thoughtful and observant to make

sure we are offering the right kind of help. We must help others in ways that are respectful of their dignity and their freedom to choose. But all around us are people who need help, and we should help them. Nothing should stop us from making a positive difference in their lives. As we read in the book of Hebrews: "God is not unjust; he will not forget your work and the love you have shown him as you have helped his people and continue to help them."[81]

Jesus called us to be people who love and help others. That's who we should be, no matter how people treat us in return.

*People really need help but may attack you if you
do help them. Help people anyway.*

Give the world the

best you have and you'll get

kicked in the teeth.

*Give the world the best
you have anyway.*

Each of us is unique, and each of us has something special to contribute. We make that contribution by always doing our best. And we *can* always do our best, because each of us controls his or her own time, attitude, and behavior. It's up to us. It's our decision.

Of course, we don't control how other people will respond when we give our best. We may give our best and get kicked in the teeth. But that is no reason to be less than we can be, or to do less than we can do. We still have to give the world our best. That is the only way we can be who we are truly meant to be.

One of my all-time favorite movies is *Chariots of Fire,* which tells the story of the British track team that went to the 1924 Paris Olympics. One of the key characters in the movie is Eric Liddell, a Scot and a devout Christian born to a missionary family in China. Liddell loved to run, his arms flailing in the air and his head tilted back. "The Lord made me fast," he told his sister. "And when I run, I feel his pleasure." Crowds came to see him run, and after he raced, he often spoke to the crowd about life and his faith in God.

The competition could be fierce, even unscrupulous. In a quarter-mile race that was held before the Olympics, Liddell was intentionally shoved off the track by another runner. He went rolling down onto the ground. For anyone else, that would have been the end of the race—but not for Liddell. He was determined to give the world his best anyway. He got up and ran the hardest he had ever run. He caught up with the other runners, and then, as the crowd went wild, he won the race. At the finish line he collapsed, his chest heaving. A track coach named Mussabini, who had watched the race, came over and knelt by Liddell as he lay on the ground, and gently raised his head. "'Twas not the prettiest quarter I've ever seen, Mr. Liddell," he said. "But certainly the bravest." Liddell continued to give the world his best. He went on to win an Olympic medal, and later returned to China as a missionary.

✦ ✦ ✦

The Old Testament story of Joseph is about giving the world your best, even when you get kicked in the teeth.

Joseph was the youngest son of Jacob. When Joseph was seventeen, Jacob made him a coat of many colors. His brothers saw the coat and knew that their father loved Joseph more than them. They began to hate Joseph. Their hatred for Joseph grew when Joseph told them about two dreams he had, dreams he interpreted to mean that his brothers and family would someday bow down to him.

When Joseph's brothers went to feed their flock in Shechem, Jacob sent Joseph to see how they were doing. When Joseph arrived, his brothers threw him into a pit and then sold him as a slave to a passing caravan of merchants on their way to Egypt. They took Joseph's coat, dipped it in the blood of a goat, and returned home to show the coat to their father. Jacob assumed that Joseph had been killed by a beast, and he wept.[82]

Joseph was purchased by Potiphar, an officer of the Pharaoh. Joseph worked hard, doing his best for his master. The Lord was with Joseph, and everything Joseph did turned out well. So Potiphar made Joseph the overseer of his house.

But Potiphar's wife found Joseph attractive, and tried to seduce him. Joseph refused to go to bed with her or even be with her. One day, when everyone else was away from the house, she grabbed him by his garment and pulled him toward her. To get away from her, Joseph left his garment in her hand and then fled. She cried out, falsely accusing him of mocking her and trying to seduce her. So Potiphar put Joseph in prison.

Joseph continued to be faithful and give his best. The keeper of the prison found favor in him, and gave him responsibility for all the other prisoners. Again, the Lord was with Joseph, and he was successful in everything he did.[83]

While in prison, Joseph interpreted the dreams of the chief butler and the chief baker, who had both been imprisoned for offending the Pharaoh. Two years later, when the Pharaoh had troubling dreams, he sought someone who could interpret them. The magicians and wise men of Egypt could not interpret the dreams, but the chief butler remembered that Joseph had accurately interpreted his own dream in prison.

So the Pharaoh sent for Joseph, who interpreted the Pharaoh's dreams. Joseph told the Pharaoh that there would be seven years of plenty, followed by seven years of famine. He urged the Pharaoh to find a discreet and wise man and put him in charge of gathering up food during the years of plenty, so that it could be stored and then eaten during the years of famine. The Pharaoh decided to appoint Joseph to do the job—to be ruler, second only to the Pharaoh himself.[84]

Joseph made sure that food was gathered and stored in the cities during the seven years of plenty. When the famine came, the Pharaoh told the people to go to Joseph, who opened the storehouses.

People from other lands came to Egypt to buy grain, because they, too, were experiencing famine. Jacob sent his sons to Egypt, where they came to Joseph, and bowed down to him. Joseph recognized his brothers, but they didn't recognize him. He tested them, and finally revealed himself to them. He told them not to be angry, because God wanted him to go to Egypt so that he could save their lives during the famine. He kissed them, and wept with them, and sent them back to Jacob with wagons full of grain and bread and meat.

The Pharaoh invited Joseph's family to reside in Egypt, where the Lord promised Jacob he would make his people into a great nation. Jacob went to Egypt, and Joseph gave his family good land. They became shepherds in Goshen.

When Jacob died, Joseph's brothers were afraid that Joseph would take revenge against them for what they had done to him so many years before. They went to Joseph, fell down before him, and said they were his slaves. But Joseph replied:

> "You intended to harm me, but God intended it for good to accomplish what is now being done, the saving of many lives. So then, don't be afraid. I will provide for you and your children." And he reassured them and spoke kindly to them.[85]

Joseph lived to be 110 years old, and saw three generations of his own children.

Joseph steadfastly gave the world the best he had. He suffered when his brothers sold him into slavery, and again when he was sent to prison. But he gave the world the best he had anyway, and the Lord made him prosper. The Israelites were preserved from the famine, and grew into a great nation.

✦ ✦ ✦

Jesus gave his best, and he, too, suffered. He died in pain on the cross. Every day, Jesus preached and performed miracles, *knowing full well* that he would suffer in the end. But he gave the world his best anyway.

Jesus knew that he was not the only one who would suffer. He knew that his followers would also suffer. He knew that his disciples would give the world their best, and get kicked in the teeth. He said: "If they persecuted me, they will persecute you also."[86] He called his disciples to take up their crosses anyway. He said that "anyone who does not take his cross and follow me is not worthy of me."[87]

When we take up our own crosses, we will be blessed with spiritual rewards. In the Beatitudes, Jesus gave us this assurance:

"Blessed are those who are persecuted because of righteousness, for theirs is the kingdom of heaven. Blessed are you when people insult you, persecute you and falsely say all kinds of evil against you because of me. Rejoice and be glad, because great is your reward in heaven, for in the same way they persecuted the prophets who were before you."[88]

Jesus did not seek martyrdom. In the garden of Gethsemane, he even said: "My Father, if it is possible, may this cup be taken from me. Yet not as I will, but as you will."[89] Jesus was not seeking to suffer. He was seeking to do God's will.

We, too, should seek to do God's will. We should seek to live as Jesus taught us to live. If living according to God's will leads to suffering, then we should not flinch. But suffering is not the goal. The goal is to be faithful.

As we live our faith, each of us will have days of discomfort, pain, and suffering; days when we are under attack; days when we feel defeated. That is when we have the best opportunity to show the world who we are and what we believe. That is when we have the best opportunity to show that we are people of God who know what is right and good and true. That is when we have the best opportunity to follow the example of Christ, loving and forgiving those who hurt us. Even in our darkest hour, we can quietly and simply carry our own crosses. Christ will be with us. He understands.

+ + +

Martin Luther King, Jr., gave the world his best, and he got kicked in the teeth. He first became involved in the civil rights movement at the beginning of the bus boycott in Montgomery, Alabama, in 1955. He was twenty-six years old. During that long boycott, he was threatened, he was arrested and jailed, and his house was bombed. During the next thirteen years, he was arrested and jailed many times, and stabbed once. Tragically, he was assassinated when he was only thirty-nine.

Throughout his nonviolent campaign for the rights of African Americans, Martin Luther King, Jr., gave the world his best. It wasn't easy. Having to live under the threat of death every day, having to take abuse and criticism, having to face so much frustration, he sometimes felt discouraged. "But then the holy spirit revives my soul again," he said in his *Autobiography*.

During his early days in Montgomery, he received a threatening phone call late one night and couldn't go back to sleep. He went to the kitchen and sat down, thinking about his wife and children, and how they might be hurt or killed. He could feel himself faltering. So he began to pray out loud at the kitchen table. In the quiet of the night, he heard an inner voice telling him to stand up for righteousness and justice and truth. In his *Autobiography,* he said, "I heard the voice of Jesus saying still to fight on," he said. "He promised never to leave me alone. At that moment I experienced the presence of the Divine as I had never experienced Him before. Almost at once my fears began to go. My uncertainty disappeared. I was ready to face anything."[90] The dangers and threats were still there, but he continued to give the world his best anyway.

As the book of Hebrews says: "Let us fix our eyes on Jesus, the author and perfecter of our faith, who for the joy set before him endured the cross, scorning its shame, and sat down at the right hand of the throne of God. Consider him who endured such opposition from sinful men, so that you will not grow weary and lose heart."[91]

James reminds us: "Blessed is the man who perseveres

under trial, because when he has stood the test, he will receive the crown of life that God has promised to those who love him."[92]

This is the life we are given. We should make the most of it. Even if things are tough and we get kicked in the teeth, we can still give the world our best. That's what Jesus did, and that's what we are here to do. It is in giving our best that we find the deepest meaning and happiness. It is in giving our best that we glorify God and grow toward the perfection that he intends for each of us.

> *Give the world the best you have and you'll get*
> *kicked in the teeth. Give the world*
> *the best you have anyway.*

Making a Difference

God wants us to be deeply happy—now, as we live each day. And he has given us all that we *need* to be deeply happy.

God created this incredible universe, abundant in resources; Christ came to teach us and save us; and the Holy Spirit is with us to inspire and encourage us. We have all that we need—the resources, the teachings, the gift of grace, and daily encouragement. It is up to us to take these gifts and live our faith. It is up to us to *do* something. As it is written in the book of James:

What good is it, my brothers, if a man claims to have faith but has no deeds? Can such faith save him? Suppose a brother or sister is without clothes and daily food. If one of you says to him, "Go, I wish you well; keep warm and well fed," but does nothing about his physical needs, what good is it? In the same way, faith by itself, if it is not accompanied by action, is dead.[93]

The Paradoxical Commandments are about action. They are about loving, and helping, and doing good *anyway*. (No excuses!)

God has given each of us many gifts. We are on this planet to use our gifts. As Peter wrote: "Each one should use whatever gift he has received to serve others, faithfully administering God's grace in its various forms."[94]

How do you serve others? How do you make a difference? Here are five ideas to keep in mind.

First, be the real you. You will make the right difference, the difference you were born to make, if you discover who you are, what gifts you have been given, and how to use those gifts to help others. You don't have to be prestigious or influential. What you have to be is *you*. You have to be the true you—the authentic you. You have to become the person that God intends you to be.

The question is not: How can you make the biggest difference? The question is: How can you make the difference that God wants you to make? You *will* make the difference God wants you to make if you discover who you are, identify the gifts God has given you, and then set forth to use those gifts in loving and helping others.

Second, since you are *in* the world, not *of* the world, don't worry about making a difference in terms of power, wealth, and fame. You may achieve these worldly symbols of success, or you may not. If you achieve them, you will see that they are simply tools to be used in loving and helping others. In the end, you will make the difference you were born to make if you are authentic, faithful, and *in* the world but not *of* the world.

Third, the difference you are called to make may be right in front of you. That is what inspires me about the story that Jesus told about the Good Samaritan. An expert in Jewish law was testing Jesus regarding the second great commandment, to love your neighbor as yourself. "And who is my neighbor?" the man asked. Jesus replied by saying:

"A man was going down from Jerusalem to Jericho, when he fell into the hands of robbers. They stripped him of his clothes, beat him and went away, leaving him half dead. A priest happened to be going down the same road, and when he saw the man, he passed by on the other side. So, too, a Levite, when he came to the place and saw him, passed by on the other side. But a Samaritan, as he traveled, came where the man was; and when he saw him, he took pity on him. He went to him and bandaged his wounds, pouring on oil and wine. Then he put the man on his own donkey, took him to an inn and took care of him. The next day he took out two silver coins and gave them to the innkeeper. 'Look after him,' he said, 'and when I return, I will reimburse you for any extra expense you may have.'"[95]

The Samaritan, of course, was the true neighbor.

What I appreciate about this story is that the Samaritan took direct, immediate action. He didn't sit down to review all the problems of the world that he might address. He didn't wonder if there was somebody else farther down the road who needed more help. He didn't say that this was a rural problem, and he was an urban specialist. He didn't interview the injured man to determine if he was worthy of help, or to determine how much help he needed, and how long he was likely to need it. He didn't ask the injured man to fill out any forms in triplicate.

No. The Samaritan saw a need, right in front of him, and he took action. He did what he could. He took the man to an inn and cared for him.

The story of the Good Samaritan is a reminder that sometimes, the difference you are called to make will be right there in front of you. You can make a difference by simply taking action.

You may need to take action immediately. That is what impresses me about the story of Abigail in the Old Testament.

David was in the desert with his men, avoiding King Saul, who wanted to kill him. Nabal was a wealthy man who lived at Carmel with his wife, Abigail. Nabal was surly and mean, but his wife, Abigail, was intelligent and beautiful.

When David learned that Nabal was shearing sheep, he sent ten young men to bear his greetings. The young men pointed out to Nabal that during the time they had been in the area, they had not mistreated Nabal's shepherds, nor had they stolen anything from them. The young men asked Nabal if he could spare anything for them, since it was a festive time.

Nabal refused to give them anything. When David heard this, he felt that he had been repaid evil for good. He was determined to kill all of Nabal's men.

One of the servants told Abigail that her husband had hurled insults at David's men, even though David's men had treated the shepherds well, and had been like a wall around them, protecting them.

Abigail acted quickly. Without telling her husband, she gathered up food and wine, loaded it on donkeys, and rode to meet David. When they met, she quickly got off her donkey, bowed down before David, apologized for her husband, and offered the food to David's men. She asked David to forgive Nabal's offense. She asked him to avoid bloodshed, so that when he became leader over Israel, he would not have on his conscience the burden of needless bloodshed and vengeance.

David praised the Lord for Abigail's actions. He accepted her gifts of food, and told her she could go home in peace.

When Abigail returned home and told Nabal what she had done, his heart failed him, and he became like a stone. Ten days later, he died. When David heard this, he sent word to Abigail, asking her to become his wife. She agreed.[96]

Abigail faced a potentially disastrous situation. She acted decisively, with courage and humility. She made a difference in her own life, and saved the lives of many others. Her story reminds us that the difference we are called to make may not only be right in front of us—we may need to take action immediately.

Fourth, you may make a difference that you did not plan to make. God may take you by surprise.

I know that God keeps taking me by surprise. The Paradoxical Commandments are the perfect example. I wrote the Paradoxical Commandments when I was nineteen, a college sophomore, back in the sixties. I was working part-time with high school student leaders all over the United States, giving speeches and writing articles about how to lead and how to reach out to one's fellow students. It occurred to me that it might help student leaders if I put all of my advice together in a booklet on leadership.

I remember sitting in my college room, a little attic space on the fifth floor of my residence hall. I sat there with my red Royal Safari manual typewriter. I remember staring at the typewriter and staring at the ceiling and staring at my hands. I spent several months debating with myself as to whether I had anything to say that would be valuable or useful to anyone. Finally, I decided to try. I decided to do it *anyway*. I didn't know what would happen. I wasn't sure that what I wrote would make a difference, but I thought it *might* make a difference. So I wrote a booklet with some ideas that were meaningful to me, hoping that they would be meaningful to student leaders as well. The Paradoxical Commandments were just part of that booklet, which was published in 1968.

While I went on with my life, the Paradoxical Commandments spread all over the world. I know now that they have been used by business executives, government officials, nonprofit leaders, military commanders, religious leaders, university presidents, teachers, social workers, athletic coaches, and students. They have been used by organizations in a wide range of countries, including the United States, Belgium, Cambodia, Canada, Hong Kong, Iran, Japan, Malaysia, South Africa, and Zimbabwe.

In September 1997, I learned that Mother Teresa had posted the Paradoxical Commandments on the wall of her children's home in Calcutta. I was deeply moved by that discovery. It had a huge impact on me. It seemed to me that God was sending me a message. The message was that I should start speaking and writing about the Paradoxical Commandments again, thirty years after I wrote them.

People are now sending me messages from all over the world, telling me how they have used the Paradoxical Commandments to raise their children, or face a crisis at work, or establish their personal goals, or improve their relationships, or keep their faith. One man wrote to tell me that a copy of the Paradoxical Commandments was the last gift his mother gave him before she died. Schoolchildren sent a copy of the Paradoxical Commandments to New York police and firefighters to encourage them in the days after 9/11. A woman wrote to tell me that her husband cherished the command-ments, which were read at his funeral. Every time she reads the commandments, she feels close to him again.

People have told me that they have carried a copy of the commandments in their wallets or purses for twenty years. Others have said that they look at the commandments every morning before going to work, to help them stay focused on what is really important. I have heard from many Christians who tell me that the commandments have reminded them to live the way Jesus wants us to live.

I had no idea that I would write something that would make a difference in the lives of so many people. I didn't know that God would make use of me in that way. I was a college sophomore in a small attic room with a manual type-writer. I wasn't trying to write something that would travel around the world. I was just hoping to be helpful to a few student leaders in the sixties. But God surprised me.

So when you set out to make a difference, just remem-ber: You may make a difference in a way you never ex-pected. God may surprise you, too!

Fifth, as you set out to make a difference in the world, remember that little things make a difference. You can change another person's life by doing something that is simple and loving. The impact can be amazing.

Mother Teresa is a wonderful example. She left her position as a teacher at a school, and went into the streets of Calcutta to help the poor. She didn't have a corporate sponsor or a government grant. In fact, she didn't know how she would make it from day to day. She started by taking care of the first hungry person she came across. And then the next one. And as she made a difference, person by person, she attracted followers and donors, and expanded her mission. She became world famous, and received the Nobel Peace Prize.

She started by doing something simple and loving. She didn't know how it would turn out. She didn't know how much of a difference she would make. But the Lord blessed her work, and it grew, until she and her Missionaries of Charity became a symbol of hope, inspiring people throughout the world to make a difference, too.

Like Mother Teresa, many Christians have stepped out in faith to make a difference in the world around them. I believe that Jesus is calling to us, offering us his hand, encouraging us to step out in faith and make the difference we were born to make.

When I find myself beginning to doubt what I can accomplish, I remind myself that Jesus was not the only one who walked on water. The apostle Peter walked on water, too.

After Jesus fed the five thousand, he sent the disciples ahead in a boat to the other side of the lake. Jesus dismissed the crowd and went up the mountainside to pray. When he finished praying, it was evening, and the boat was far from the shore, buffeted by wind and waves.

During the fourth watch of the night Jesus went out to them, walking on the lake. When the disciples saw him walking on the lake, they were terrified. "It's a ghost," they said, and cried out in fear.

But Jesus immediately said to them: "Take courage! It is I. Don't be afraid."

"Lord, if it's you," Peter replied, "tell me to come to you on the water."

"Come," he said.

Then Peter got down out of the boat, walked on

the water and came toward Jesus. But when he saw the wind, he was afraid and, beginning to sink, cried out, "Lord, save me!"

Immediately Jesus reached out his hand and caught him. "You of little faith," he said, "why did you doubt?"[97]

Peter walked on water *when he had faith and walked toward Jesus.* If we have faith and walk toward Jesus, we will be amazed at what we can accomplish, too. And if we have moments of fear and begin to sink, Jesus will reach out and catch us.

One reason that we must step out in faith is that we can't see the whole picture. We don't know where all the pieces fit, and why everything happens the way it does. We see through a glass, darkly. Only God knows what it all means. Only God knows the impact of each of our actions and each of our prayers.

As a result, you will not see or understand every difference that you make during your lifetime. But this should not discourage you. If you love God, and love your neighbor as yourself—if you live the two Great Commandments—you *will* make a difference. It's going to happen, even if you can't see it or understand it. If you spend your life loving and helping others as Jesus taught us to do, you will create ripples. You can be confident that those ripples will make a difference, even if you don't know how big they are, or how far they will go, or who they will ultimately touch.

James wrote: "Anyone, then, who knows the good he ought to do and doesn't do it, sins."[98] So take action. Let your faith flow into your deeds. Use the gifts God has given you. If you do, you will surely make a difference. You will fulfill your purpose, and find meaning and deep happiness. You will be blessed, and you will be a blessing to others.

To God be the glory!

Will You Answer the Call?

Jesus is calling you to a paradoxical life.

He is not calling you to worldly success. He is calling you to serve God.

He is calling you to be in the world, not of the world.

He is calling you to love and help people, no matter what.

He is calling you to reach out to those in need and make a difference now.

You may have worldly riches, or you may not. But you can always enjoy the richness of a life with God.

You may have worldly power, or you may not. But you can always experience the power of Christ.

You may have worldly fame, or you may not. But you can always be known to the Holy Spirit.

You may lose your way, or you may not. But you can always walk with God.

You may suffer, or you may not. But you can always find deep happiness in Christ.

You may know fear, or you may not. But you can always find encouragement in the Holy Spirit.

Jesus is calling you to a paradoxical life.

Will you answer his call?

Jesus did it anyway.

Will you?

Sources

1. Ecclesiastes 2:4–11.

2. Ecclesiastes 2:22–23.

3. Ecclesiastes 5:10.

4. Ecclesiastes 7:15.

5. Ecclesiastes 9:11.

6. Ecclesiastes 3:12–13.

7. Ecclesiastes 12:13.

8. John 17:14–15.

9. Romans 12:2.

10. Matthew 4:10; see also Luke 4:8.

11. Matthew 20:25–28; see also Mark 10:42–45.

12. Luke 12:15.

13. Matthew 6:19–21, 24; see also Luke 12:33–34 and Luke 16:13.

14. Matthew 19:21–24; see also Mark 10:21–25.

15. Matthew 20:26–27.

16. Matthew 20:16.

17. Matthew 18:3.

18. Matthew 10:39; see also Mark 8:35.

19. Matthew 5:3–10.

20. Luke 23:34.

21. Luke 15:11–31.

22. Matthew 22:37–40; see also Mark 12:29–31, Luke 10:27–28.

23. John 13:34–35.

24. 1 John 4:7–8.

25. 1 Samuel 17:28.

26. 2 Samuel 16:7–8.

27. 2 Samuel 16:12.

28. Luke 23:2.

29. 1 Peter 2:20–21.

30. 1 Peter 3:13–17.

31. Galatians 6:9–10.

32. Genesis 26:1–6, 12–22.

33. Judges 13:5.

34. Judges 16:17.

35. Judges 16:18–21.

36. Judges 16:30.

37. Luke 22:3–4.

38. Exodus 7:1 to 13:22.

39. Deuteronomy 34:10–12.

40. Exodus 14:11–12.

41. Exodus 14:31.

42. Exodus 16:3.

43. Exodus 17:3–4.

44. Exodus 32:1.

45. Exodus 32:4.

46. Matthew 21:9.

47. Ephesians 2:10.

48. Esther 2:1–17.

49. Esther 3:1–14.

50. Esther 4:7–11.

51. Esther 5:1–14.

52. Esther 7:1–10.

53. John 10:23–31.

54. Matthew 23:13–33.

55. Matthew 23:27–28.

56. Ephesians 4:15.

57. Ephesians 4:25.

58. Albert Schweitzer, *Pilgrimage to Humanity* (New York: The Wisdom Library, 1961), pp. 15–16.

59. Daniel 6:1–11.

60. Daniel 6:21–22.

61. Daniel 6:25–27.

62. Luke 4:29.

63. Matthew 13:58.

64. Matthew 9:10–13.

65. Matthew 21:28–32.

66. Matthew 25:31–46.

67. Matthew 25:40.

68. Job 1:1–3.

69. Job 1:21.

70. Job 2:9.

71. Job 2:10.

72. Acts 18:1–11.

73. 1 Corinthians 13; 1 Corinthians 15.

74. 1 Samuel 16:14–23.

75. 1 Samuel 17:32–51.

76. 1 Samuel 19:4–5.

77. 1 Samuel 24:11–12.

78. John 3:1–2.

79. John 12:42.

80. Mark 12:28–34.

81. Hebrews 6:10.

82. Genesis 37:3–35.

83. Genesis 39:1–23.

84. Genesis 40:1 to 41:41.

85. Genesis 50:20–21.

86. John 15:20.

87. Matthew 10:38.

88. Matthew 5:10–12.

89. Matthew 26:39; see also Mark 14:36, Luke 22:42.

90. Clayborne Carson, ed., *The Autobiography of Martin Luther King, Jr.* (New York: Intellectual Properties Management/ Warner Books, 1998), pp. 76–78.

91. Hebrews 12:2–3.

92. James 1:12.

93. James 2:14–17.

94. 1 Peter 4:10.

95. Luke 10:30–35.

96. 1 Samuel 25:2–42.

97. Matthew 14:25–31.

98. James 4:17

STUDY GUIDE

INTRODUCTION

1. Do you yearn for a more meaningful life?

2. In what areas or aspects of your life have you found the most meaning? How do those areas or aspects relate to your faith?

3. Have you sought meaning in power, wealth, fame, or physical pleasure? If so, did you find any? If not, why not?

4. What does the book of Ecclesiastes say about power, wealth, fame, and physical pleasure?

5. The voice in Ecclesiastes describes specific pleasures,

such as houses, planted vineyards, gardens, parks, reservoirs of water, slaves, herds and flocks, silver and gold, singers, and a harem. What pleasures would appear on today's list?

6. Do you agree that whoever loves money never has enough, and whoever loves wealth is never satisfied with his income? Why?

7. Have you ever seen a righteous person perish, or be punished or neglected?

8. Do you think the world is fair or just? If so, why? If not, why not?

9. What does Ecclesiastes say is meaningful?

10. Do you agree that deep, lasting happiness doesn't come from the world around us, but from our relationship with God? Have you experienced this kind of deep, lasting happiness?

11. What achievements in your life felt "empty" to you afterward? What was the situation? What was missing?

12. Who in your life is an example of someone who has truly lived a meaningful, happy life? How do they live?

13. How did the coming of Christ add to the message of Ecclesiastes?

The Call

1. Do you believe that God wants us to be deeply happy? Why? Why not?

2. What does "deep happiness" mean to you?

3. Reflect on times you have experienced deep happiness. What was the situation? Who was involved? How did you feel? And what made these moments of deep happiness different from times that simply felt good? How did those times relate to your faith?

4. What in "The Call" is appealing to you? Why?

5. What in "The Call" is hard for you? Why?

In the World, Not of the World

1. Why did Jesus say that the world hated him and his disciples?

2. In his prayer to his Father during the Last Supper, how did Jesus describe his disciples? What did Jesus ask his Father to do for his disciples?

3. Describe all the ways that Jesus was *in* the world.

4. In what ways are you *in* the world?

5. In his prayer, Jesus said that he was not *of* the world. How did he demonstrate that when he was tempted in the desert by the devil? In what other ways did he demonstrate through his ministry that he was not *of* the world?

6. In what ways are you *of* the world? Why? Can you change?

7. In what ways are you not *of* the world? Why?

8. What did Jesus say about wealth and power? (See Matthew 6:19–24, 19:16–24, and 20:25–28, and Mark 10:17–25 and 10:42–45.)

9. In Romans 12:2, Paul said that we shouldn't conform to

the ways of the world. What pressures do you feel to conform? What did Paul say we should do instead of conforming to the ways of the world?

10. If Jesus is not calling us to be "successful" in the worldly sense, what is he calling us to?

11. Can Christians find meaning and deep happiness in the life of the Spirit and *also* have wealth and power?

12. What would your life be like if you were living *in* the world but not *of* the world? How would other people describe you? How would you feel about yourself?

13. Each Paradoxical Commandment begins with a statement of adversity, followed by a positive commandment. What is the paradox?

14. What paradoxes did Jesus use to help us see the kingdom of God?

15. Do you agree that we can control our inner lives? What is going on right now in your inner life? What action might you take today to obey and celebrate the inner life that Jesus is calling you to?

16. Which of the Beatitudes resonates most strongly with you today?

17. Which of the Beatitudes is easiest for you to accept? Which is the hardest? Why?

18. Have you known the peace of God? If so, think of times you have experienced it. How would you describe it? Who was with you, in spirit or in flesh? What made it special? How can you experience it again?

THE MESSAGE OF GOOD FRIDAY

1. Have you ever felt overwhelmed by the cruelty, pain, and hate in the world? Have you ever been really down and alone? Share what it was like.

2. How do you keep going, when you feel overwhelmed by the negative forces around you?

3. Do you know individuals who have risen above their pain and suffering? How did they do it? Are you capable of rising above?

4. How did Jesus respond to the cruelty, pain, and hate on Good Friday? What did he teach us through his actions that day?

5. Read what the scriptures say about Christ's time on the cross: Matthew 27:32–56, Mark 15:23–41, Luke 23:26–49, and John 19:16–37. What do these passages say to you about your life as a Christian?

6. In following the example of Jesus on Good Friday, what steps could you take today to respond to negative forces in your life?

7. Do you believe that if we are strong in our faith, the world can't change us, and we can still be who we are meant to be?

8. What help do we need to live the Paradoxical Commandments? Where can the strength come from?

THE PARADOXICAL COMMANDMENTS

#1. People are illogical, unreasonable, and self-centered. Love them anyway.

1. Put this commandment into your own words.

2. Is it hard or easy to live this commandment? Give examples.

3. In the parable of the prodigal son, which son do you identify with?

4. If you were the father in the story, which son would you find it easiest to love anyway?

5. Have you ever withheld your love from someone important to you? How did you feel at the time? How did you feel later?

6. Is there someone you once thought was unlovable, but whom you now love? How did you come to love that person?

7. Have you experienced being loved by others when you were illogical, unreasonable, and self-centered?

8. Have you experienced unconditional love? If so, what was/is it like?

9. Was there someone who had "nice words" for you when you were a child? What influence has that had on your life?

10. What "nice words" do you share with those you love?

11. Jesus commanded his disciples to love one another as he loved them. How did Jesus love them?

12. Can you love your enemies? If so, is it difficult? Why? Why not?

13. Who are the enemies Jesus wants you to love right now? What are two or three small steps you can take toward loving them?

14. When it comes to loving others, did Jesus allow any excuses?

15. In the New Testament there are more than twenty verses urging us to love others. Can you find the verses?

16. Read 1 Corinthians 13. What does it say to you today? What phrases touch your heart?

17. Do you agree that love is what Christian life is about? Why? Why not?

18. Do you agree that "If we do not love others, we miss God's purpose for our lives"?

19. How does your faith help you to live this commandment?

#2. If you do good, people will accuse you of selfish ulterior motives. Do good anyway.

1. Put this commandment into your own words.

2. Have you ever been accused of selfish ulterior motives? Was the accusation correct or false?

3. If you were accused of selfish ulterior motives and the accusation was false, how did it make you feel?

4. How do you respond to people who unjustly accuse you of selfish ulterior motives?

5. How did David feel when he was accused of selfish ulterior motives? What did he do or say?

6. What selfish ulterior motives was Jesus accused of by the Jewish leaders? Did Jesus respond? If so, how?

7. Who do you know who is often attacked for having ulterior motives that you feel are not true? What could you do to support that person?

8. Reflect on 1 Peter 2:20–21 and 1 Peter 3:13–17. What did Peter say about suffering when you do good?

9. Reflect on Galatians 6:9–10. Why did Paul say that we should not become weary in doing good?

10. If you are accused of selfish ulterior motives and you do good anyway, how do you feel?

11. How does your faith help you to live this commandment?

#3. If you are successful, you will win false friends and true enemies. Succeed anyway.

1. Put this commandment into your own words.

2. Are you jealous when others are successful? Why? Why not?

3. Have others been jealous of you when you were successful? Why? Why not?

4. Have you ever had a "false friend"? If so, how did that make you feel?

5. How do you know when a friend has become a "false friend"?

6. If you have had a false friend, how did you treat that person after you discovered that she or he was being false to your friendship? Were you able to transform that false friend into a true friend?

7. Did Delilah start out as a false friend of Samson, or did she change from a true friend to a false one?

8. Did Judas start out as a false friend of Jesus, or did he change from a true friend to a false one?

9. How do you know when a friend is a "true friend"?

10. Have you ever had a true enemy? If so, how did you deal with him or her?

11. If you have had a true enemy, what did you learn about him or her? What did the experience of having a true enemy teach you about yourself?

12. How have your family and true friends supported you in your journey?

13. What do you think motivates a person to be a false friend or a true enemy? What might be going on in his or her life?

14. What are the gifts that God has given you? How do you use them?

15. In just one sentence, summarize the purpose of your life.

16. Why should you succeed anyway?

17. How does your faith help you to live this commandment?

#4. *The good you do today will be forgotten tomorrow. Do good anyway.*

1. Put this commandment into your own words.

2. How important is it to you to be recognized for your good works?

3. Have you ever done a good deed for another that was soon forgotten? If so, how did you react? Were you angry or discouraged? Did you feel sorry for yourself? Did you come to dislike the other person, and decide to avoid that person or get even with that person? Or did you accept the situation and maintain a positive relationship with the other person?

4. If you did a good deed that was forgotten, did that change in any way how you felt about the good deed you did?

5. Why do people forget the good that others do for them?

6. Why do people forget the good that God does for them?

7. What good things have been done to you that you should remember? How can you show that you remember? Who can you call or write to, today, to let them know that you remember and appreciate what they did for you?

8. When it comes to family, friends, or colleagues, do you ever catch yourself thinking, "What have they done for me lately?"

9. What good things have you done that you forgot about for years, then one day remembered again? How did it feel when you remembered?

10. When you do good things that go totally unnoticed by others, do you feel particularly close to God at that moment?

11. Why did Moses continue to faithfully lead the Israelites, even when they kept forgetting the good he and God did for them?

12. Why did Jesus continue to teach, and heal, and reach out to the outcast, even when he knew that people would forget the good he did?

13. Would you have gone to the funeral that Jack Brady went to? Why or why not? If you went, how would you have felt?

14. Who always knows the good we do, and never forgets?

15. What good things are you doing today?

16. How does your faith help you to live this commandment?

#5. Honesty and frankness make you vulnerable.
Be honest and frank anyway.

1. Put this commandment into your own words.

2. Have you been in a situation in which your honesty and

frankness made you vulnerable? If so, what did you do? How did you feel about your decision? How did your decision affect others?

3. Have you ever been dishonest in order to keep a job or a friendship? If so, what was the result? Did it change in any way how you felt about yourself? Did it change your relationship with others?

4. Would you have done what Elizabeth did in the story about the Romanian Commission on Adoptions? Why? Why not?

5. Esther was honest and frank. What were some of her other qualities that were crucial in her story?

6. Why was Jesus so honest and frank with the scribes and Pharisees? Why didn't he maintain silence?

7. What role does honesty play in building strong, positive, caring relationships? Why?

8. Have you ever broken the trust of another, especially a loved one? What happened? Were you able to restore that trust? How?

9. What does it mean to you to "speak the truth in love" (Ephesians 4:15)?

10. Think of times in your life when you have spoken the truth in love, when you have spoken the truth harshly, and when you have held back the truth in love. How did each feel? What did others do when you spoke in each of these three different ways?

11. Reflect on a time when someone was honest and frank with you about a weakness or undesirable trait. How did he or she share the truth with you? How did you feel toward that person? How did you feel about your-self? Did you grow as a person?

12. Have you ever been honest and frank with someone about his or her weaknesses or undesirable traits? If so, how did you share the truth with him or her? How did that person feel toward you? How did you feel about yourself? Do you think your honesty and frankness helped the other person to grow?

13. How does your faith help you to live this command-ment?

#6. The biggest men and women with the biggest ideas can be shot down by the smallest men and women with the smallest minds. Think big anyway.

1. Put this commandment into your own words.

2. What is the biggest idea you have ever had? Was it a big idea because of the simple truth at its core? Was it big because it was universal in application and could affect a lot of people?

3. Have you ever had a "big idea" that was shot down by someone else? If so, how did you feel? How did you respond? Did it affect your relationship with that other person?

4. Have you ever been a "small person" who tried to shoot down someone else's big ideas? If so, why did you do it?

5. Name some "big men and women" with some "big ideas" who thought big anyway—and succeeded.

6. Who in your life had a big idea that had an important influence on you?

7. What made Daniel a "big man" with "big ideas"? Why did the administrators and subordinates want to shoot him down?

8. Why was Jesus rejected in his own hometown?

9. Have you ever succeeded in doing something that others said could not be done? What gave you the strength and courage to persevere? What did you learn about yourself from that experience?

10. What big ideas do you have now? What are you doing about them?

11. Why should you think big anyway, no matter what anybody else says?

12. How does your faith help you to live this commandment?

#7. People favor underdogs, but follow only top dogs. Fight for a few underdogs anyway.

1. Put this commandment into your own words.

2. Who are the underdogs in your family, your church, your organization, or your community?

3. Do you see yourself as an underdog? If so, why? If not, why not?

4. Do you sympathize with underdogs? Why? Which ones?

5. Was there a time in your life when you felt like an underdog and somebody reached out to you? Reflect on what you learned from that experience.

6. Have you ever taken the risk of supporting an underdog? If so, what was it like? If not, why not?

7. Who do you know, right now, who helps outcasts and outsiders?

8. Why did Jesus care about underdogs? How did he behave toward them?

9. In the parable of the sheep and the goats, Jesus said that when we feed the hungry, give drink to the thirsty, provide hospitality to strangers, clothe the naked, look after the sick, and visit those in prison, we are doing it for him. Do you do these things? If so, explain. If not, why not?

10. Utu Langi drove past the man who was cold and needed a blanket. Then he changed his mind and went back. What would you do? Why?

11. Why is it easier to follow top dogs than to fight for underdogs?

12. Why should you fight for a few underdogs anyway?

13. Which underdogs need your help today?

14. How does your faith help you to live this commandment?

#8. What you spend years building may be destroyed overnight. Build anyway.

1. Put this commandment into your own words.

2. What are you trying to build in your life, your family, your community, your world?

3. What is the most important thing that you have built in your life so far?

4. Have you ever lost something that you spent years building? If so, did you build again anyway?

5. What have you lost that was hardest to live without? Why?

6. Think of a time in your life when a calamity struck. Did your family, friends, and neighbors pull together?

7. Do you know someone who seems to have given up af-

ter a major setback in life? If so, what might you do to help that person decide to build again anyway?

8. Job cursed his fate, but he didn't curse God. Do you make that distinction when something bad happens to you?

9. Psalm 127:1 says: "Unless the Lord builds the house, its builders labor in vain." What does that mean in our world today?

10. Reflect on the meaning of Jesus' story about the house built on a rock (Matthew 7:24–27).

11. What do you have that can never be taken away from you?

12. What can always be stronger than any calamity or disaster?

13. How does your faith help you to live this commandment?

#9. People really need help but may attack you if you do help them. Help people anyway.

1. Put this commandment into your own words.

2. Have you ever tried to help someone, and been attacked by that person? If so, how did you feel? What did you do?

3. If you have been attacked by someone you were trying to help, why do you think the person did it? Was the attack really about you, or was it about something happening in that person's life instead?

4. Have you ever attacked somebody who was helping you? If so, why did you do it? What was the outcome?

5. Why did Saul want to kill David?

6. Why did David continue to help Saul anyway?

7. Why did Jesus try to reach the Jewish leaders and Pharisees with his message?

8. Why did the Jewish leaders want to kill Jesus?

9. Are you willing to help someone who really needs help but may not be appreciative? If so, why? If not, why not?

10. Why should you help people anyway?

11. How does your faith help you to live this commandment?

#10. Give the world the best you have and you'll get kicked in the teeth. Give the world the best you have anyway.

1. Put this commandment into your own words.

2. Who are you and what are you doing when you are giving the world your best? How does it make you feel?

3. Do you agree that you can always give your best? If so, why? If not, why not?

4. Who has touched your life by always giving his or her best?

5. Have you ever helped somebody else to discover their gifts and give the world their best? How did that make you feel?

6. Jesus said: "Be perfect, therefore, as your heavenly Father is perfect" (Matthew 5:48). What does this mean to you today?

7. Have you ever given the world your best, and gotten kicked in the teeth? How did it feel? How did you respond?

8. Why did Joseph continue to give the world his best, even when he got kicked in the teeth?

9. Jesus suffered, and he knew that his followers would also suffer. Why did he call on his disciples to take up their crosses and follow him?

10. What opportunities do we have when we are suffering, or under attack, or feeling defeated?

11. What is the best way to get through a period of suffering or trial? What inner resources are available to you?

12. Why should we always give the world our best anyway?

13. How does your faith help you to live this commandment?

Making a Difference

1. Do you agree that God has given us all that we need, so now it is up to us to do something?

2. What gifts do you believe that you have been given? (Name at least three.) Have you been able to use these gifts? If so, how? If not, why not?

3. Are you the real you—the authentic you, the you that God intends you to be? If so, what helps you to be you? If not, what keeps you from being you?

4. Are you being called to make a difference that is right in front of you, like the Good Samaritan?

5. Have you ever been in Abigail's shoes, and had to take action quickly, with courage and humility?

6. Did you ever make a difference that you didn't plan to make? (Did God take you by surprise?)

7. What little things can you do that will make a difference?

8. Does it matter that we can't see the whole picture, and only God knows the impact of each of our actions and prayers?

9. Do you agree with James that failing to act is a sin?

10. When you look back on your life so far, do you have more regrets about the things you did or the things you didn't do?

11. Who has made a difference in your life?

12. How can you make a difference in someone else's life right now? Are you committed to doing it?

13. Is there anything in your life you need to change, in order to make the difference that God wants you to make?

14. Reflect on the story of Peter walking on the water toward Jesus (Matthew 14:25–31). What can you do to strengthen your faith and walk toward Jesus?

WILL YOU ANSWER THE CALL?

1. Do you believe that whatever happens, you can always enjoy the richness of life with God?
2. Do you believe that whatever happens, you can always experience the power of Christ?
3. Do you believe that whatever happens, you can always be known to the Holy Spirit?
4. Do you believe that even if you lose your way, or suffer, or know fear, you can always walk with God, and find deep happiness in Christ, and find encouragement in the Holy Spirit?
5. Do you hear Jesus calling you to a paradoxical life?
6. Will you answer his call? Will you do it *anyway*?

Acknowledgments

All quotations of scripture are from the New International Version of the Holy Bible, unless otherwise noted. I want to thank Zondervan Bible Publishers for permission to quote extensively.

I first began working on "The Paradoxical Commandments for Christians" for a Sunday School class that I presented to adults at Manoa Valley Church in the fall of 2003. I want to thank Nobue Izutsu and the members of the class for their encouragement and support.

While many people had asked me for Bible stories and verses that illustrate the Paradoxical Commandments, what spurred me to write this book was an interview with Dr. Robert H. Schuller at the Crystal Cathedral in Garden Grove, California, in March 2004. He asked me to explain how the Paradoxical Commandments relate to the Bible and the Christian faith. I was able to give him a short answer, and then decided to write a complete answer in the form of this book.

The chapter on the message of Good Friday is based on my presentation as the keynote speaker at the Good Friday Breakfast hosted by the Anaheim Family YMCA in 2004. A week speaking in Marion, Indiana, as the guest of Project Leadership at Indiana Wesleyan University gave me time and a wonderful environment for writing. Jack Brady and Dawn Brown inspired me with their work and their faith.

I am very grateful to the following friends who read and commented on the manuscript: Carl Ashizawa; the Reverend Don Asman; the Reverend John Bolin, S.M.; Patrick Bolton; Jack Brady; the Reverend Dan Chun; Jerry Glashagel; the Reverend Dan Hatch; Nobue Izutsu; Evelyn Keith; Kristina Keith; Greg Kemp; Mark Kerr; Linda Kramer; the Reverend Nelson Kwon; the Reverend Scott Lewis, S.J.; the Reverend Alan Mark; Les Miyamoto; the Reverend

Robert Morgan; Dr. Fran Newman; Dr. Sheryl Nojima; Caroline Ward Oda; Mary Tikalsky; Charlotte Walters; Dr. John Westerdahl; August Yee; and Dr. Takeshi Yoshihara. Special thanks to the Reverend Don Asman, Jerry Glashagel, the Reverend Dan Hatch, and the Reverend Nelson Kwon for suggesting questions for the study guide. I thank my wife, Elizabeth Keith, for her comments on the text and for being such a blessing in my life.

I send my heartfelt thanks to my agents, Roger Jellinek and Eden-Lee Murray of the Jellinek & Murray Literary Agency, for their excellent advice and friendship during the development of this book. It has been a privilege to work with the wonderful team at G. P. Putnam's Sons—Susan Petersen Kennedy, Ivan Held, Dan Harvey, Dick Heffernan, Mike Brennan, Paul Deykerhoff, John Lawton, Stephanie Sorensen, Inga Fairclough, Andrea Ho, Allison Hargraves, Diana Meunier, Amanda Dewey, and Christine Pepe, my enthusiastic, thoughtful, and skillful editor. I thank God for the way He has smiled on me through all the people who have assisted me in preparing this book for publication.

Notes

Notes

Notes

Notes

Notes

Notes